P9-AZV-399

AMERICA
THE
EDIBLE

★ ★ ★

ADAM RICHMAN

AMERICA
THE
EDIBLE

A Hungry History,
from Sea to Dining Sea

ADAM RICHMAN

RODALE

Mention of specific companies, organizations, or authorities
in this book does not imply endorsement by the author or publisher,
nor does mention of specific companies, organizations, or authorities imply
that they endorse this book, its author, or the publisher.

Internet addresses and telephone numbers given in this book
were accurate at the time it went to press.

© 2010 by Adam Richman

All rights reserved. No part of this publication may be reproduced
or transmitted in any form or by any means, electronic or mechanical, including
photocopying, recording, or any other information storage and retrieval system,
without the written permission of the publisher.

Rodale books may be purchased for business or promotional
use or for special sales. For information, please write to:
Special Markets Department, Rodale Inc., 733 Third Avenue, New York, NY 10017

Printed in the United States of America
Rodale Inc. makes every effort to use acid-free ⊗, recycled paper ♻.

Book design by Christopher Rhoads
Cover photos: Adam Richman photographed by Peter Murphy
at M. Wells Diner, Long Island City, NY

Library of Congress Cataloging-in-Publication Data
Richman, Adam
    America the edible : a hungry history, from sea to dining sea / Adam Richman.
        p.   cm.
    ISBN-13 978–1–60529–302–8 hardcover
    1. Cooking, American. 2. Cooking—United States. I. Title.
TX715.R5586   2010
641.5973—dc22   2010039636

Distributed to the trade by Macmillan
2   4   6   8   10   9   7   5   3   1   hardcover

We inspire and enable people to improve their lives and the world around them.

This is for the eaters,
the lovers,
the livers, and the liars.

For my
friends, my family,
and for you.

CONTENTS

CONTENTS

INTRODUCTION

America the Edible is a collection of love letters to some of my favorite food places, their histories, and the time I spent there. It is an admittedly idiosyncratic survey. These cities are a pastiche of the places I've lived, places work has taken me, places wanderlust and fate have plopped me in the middle of. There was no particular rhyme or reason to their selection, merely the fact that I have had wonderful and varied food experiences in each.

It is also, if I'm to be honest with myself as well as you, dear reader, a little bit of an examination of appetites both gastronomic and otherwise. When I look back at the great bites I've encountered throughout my life, it has always been the context, the companionship, all the wonderful ancillary bips and bops that have shaped the excellence of the meal. Food on its own can do only so much to be transportive; it's when you add the seasoning provided by a loved (or loathed) one across the table and the circumstances that brought you there that a meal becomes truly memorable (for better or worse).

When I started a food journal in college (which not only helped me land the gig on *Man v. Food*, but also became the basis for the

 book in your hands), it was after a monster breakup. I found myself at a small place I'd discovered in Atlanta, and the waitress's kindness and the music that was playing became as much a part of the experience and the memory as the food on my plate. And I think that's true for most of us: The people we share an experience with become part of that experience. Those meals, those times, would not have been nearly as delicious without them.

I initially conceived of this book as an accessible, nondogmatic, non-douchey guide to the culinary anthropology of a handful of American cities, some known as culinary giants and others without such lauded food identities.

I've long been intrigued by the notion of culinary anthropology. When I was a struggling actor supporting myself by working in the restaurant industry, I saw an episode of a cooking show that featured a culinary anthropologist. Her knowledge and her perspective on food blew me away; realizing that one could connect the study of humanity with what a particular group of people ate, how their foods were named, and how they were served made me look at the edible world around me in a whole new way. When examined through the lens of culinary anthropology, a dish becomes an edible manifestation of the wars, immigrations, weather patterns, and agricultural practices that shaped it—all in one tasty, bite-size

Things No Foodie Traveller Should Be Without

1. Antacid (I'm partial to Zantac)
2. Hand sanitizer gel (especially if you're doing street food)
3. Napkins or a wet wipe or two because they *don't* always put "napkins in the bag"
4. A journal—write *everything* down!
5. Mints—not just in case of bad breath, but also for times (like when a dish sucks) when you want to cleanse your palate ASAFP! I like Listerine PocketPak strips

morsel. For that reason, whenever I am eating in a new town (and I am often eating in a new town), I make it a point to patronize local, independent places with dishes that speak to the personal histories of those who create and serve them. So that was my initial impulse—a tome of culinary anthro from a kid who learned most of what he knows about the topic at the Brooklyn Public Library.

But when I started to winnow down the cities I wanted to write about to a manageable number, I realized that it was the firsthand experiences more than the histories and the statistics that really brought the "food story" of a place to life. I have always been peripatetic by nature, following girls, jobs, and acting gigs literally from coast to coast and from north to south. My TV career and a new love took me to Austin, my theater career took me to St. Louis, my mom's womb took me to Brooklyn, a girlfriend's dad took me to Hawaii, and on it goes. It was on these journeys that I made the culinary discoveries that I recorded in that food journal (which I still continue to this day). It was not a collection of jaded, antiseptic reviews, but a collection of facts, thoughts, even photos, in which I attempted to capture the feel of a place as much as its fare. And in the final analysis, the feel is what really counts, what endures. These places left their marks on me and I, in turn, dove into them face-first, fork-first, tasting the foods beside the locals who eat them every day, in some cases meeting descen-

dants of the people who created and named the very dishes we were eating. And it was the discovery of these places—being open to whatever came my way, whether it was great food, a bad lover, wild music, or warm beer, keeping the channel clear, my eyes and heart open, and honest discourse going with myself— that kept me grounded, hungry for more, and able to suck the marrow out of moments as well as succulent roasted bones. Whether I got to these places through a suggestion from a friend, a wrong turn, or a twist of fate—that was also part of the story. As were, in many cases, my dinner companions.

I live a life propelled by what a writer once described as the "velocity of travel." I am grateful that landing the job as host on *Man v. Food* has allowed me the opportunity not only to see so much of this great, great country, but also to sample some of its finest foods, meet some of its greatest homespun cooks, and learn more about the history and, more importantly, about the humanity behind incredible foods in unlikely or unexpected places.

My dogged pursuit of new and different food experiences, whenever and wherever they are to be found, has led to all kinds of interactions everywhere, at unlikely times, with unlikely people, unlikely foods, and unlikely results. At times when I've been lost, food, friends, and fate have helped show me the way home—wherever home was at that time.

This book presents snapshots of nine American cities and some of the foods that have stood the test of time, not only as delicious contributions to these places but also as mouthwatering milestones in my life and indelible reminders of my time spent there. A foodie's tour of each city's culinary heart while wearing his own on his sleeve.

Hopefully, in the following pages you'll get a more immersive, real-world impression of these cities, their foods, and their culinary souls through the eyes of one particular fella and his ups, downs, heartaches, and hamburgers. Me and the food—both changed by the people we've come in contact with, changing with the seasons, influenced by our backgrounds and how we're presented.

With love, thanks, and gratitude for this wonderful life, I hope these accounts of my travels lead you on delicious journeys of your own.

—A.R.

AMERICA
THE
EDIBLE

★ ★ ★

ADAM RICHMAN

✫ ✫ ✫

CHAPTER 1

A LEFT-COAST LIFE, PART I

Beyond Sprouts, Pilates, and Orange Iced Tea

✫ ✫ ✫

LOS ANGELES, CA

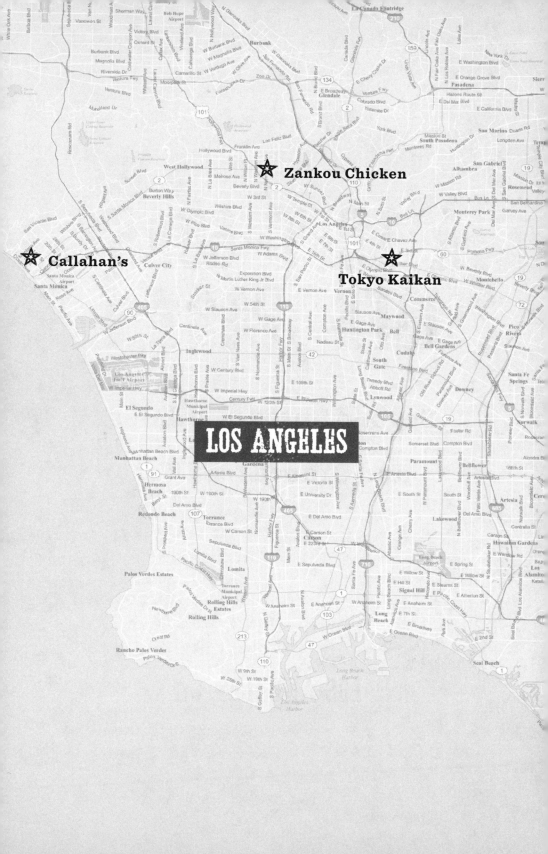

It is morning. It is 2004.

I wake up on an air mattress in a near-empty room in mid-Wilshire.

Palm fronds do a frenetic interpretive dance in the late morning half-light streaming through the vertical blinds.

I gaze around my room.

The rolltop desk left by the previous occupant is loaded with sides (short pieces from scripts that actors use to prepare for auditions) for roles that I am up for, callbacks, and the near-misses where I just couldn't figure out what the hell went wrong. There are also reams of paperwork from two of my "survival" jobs, neither of which I am working today.

No, today is the real *work.*

It is an audition day.

Game on.

Waking up had been hard these days. I was working four jobs and was barely able to get by. I'd moved three times since I'd been out here, been screwed by landlords and Craigslisters alike, and a week ago my roommate foolishly totaled my car while fucking parking it.

I'd been sucker punched, stolen from, and three days before I left to drive out here, the girl who was the center of my universe broke my heart. One day into my solo cross-country drive, I called her as I was about to cross the Rockies. I told her I would hang a hard right and come to her in Minnesota to give it another try, as distance had been our enemy. The last thing I heard before I lost the signal:

"I don't love you anymore."

I came out on the other side of the mountains and saw I had reception again, but no voice mail from the girl. At just that moment I got a call. It was the job I was to have had waiting for me. They had downsized. There was no more job.

No job, no girl, and half the country still to go.

California, here I come. Whoop-de-do.

I had left for LA knowing I had a handful of friends here. Somehow, they'd all gone on vacation at once—not sure when they'd be back.

And Grandpa died a month ago.

Yup, gravity had me by the balls and seemed to be doing chin-ups on them. Waking up was hard.

I stretched all my limbs at once, groaned like I was being exorcised, and rolled onto the floor to the left of the bed.

Fifty push-ups.

One-minute bridge.

Up to seven sun salutations.

Down to cobra stretch.

Roll over. Pilates "hundreds."

Fifty leg raises.

A hundred crunches.

Twenty-five twisting crunches to either side.

Back bridge.

Lie on floor and curse.

The day's audition was for a role as a New York lawyer from the streets with smarts but a still-streetwise edge. I got sent out for every New York role out here.

I took my well-worn, much-repaired suit into the bathroom with me so the steam from the shower could get the old bitch camera ready.

I warmed up my voice in the shower, which probably sounded like mating camels.

I shaved.

I dressed.

I made a protein shake with egg white and whey for breakfast—the whole time cursing the delicious bacon-and-egg smells emanating from the IHOP next door.

I went to the garage and hopped into my insurance-provided rental, which I had to say was a pretty cool upgrade on my own car. In LA, you are what you drive, and though I may feel like it most of the time, I don't want the world knowing I'm a beat-up Dodge Neon.

I checked my Thomas Guide for directions to Culver City, where I was to audition for major TV casting director Eileen Stringer. I had recognized her name when my agents gave me my sides, and I wanted to impress her, if not enough for this project, then enough that she would keep me in mind for future roles.

I reviewed my sides again. I went over my lines backward and forward—trying to be as "small" and natural as possible, trying to use my damn master's degree and pursue an objective, as they taught me—to treat today like a performance. For once to have one damn thing go right out here.

I hung my jacket on a hanger in the backseat, pulled on my shades, and pulled out into the cheesecloth of the smog-covered city, headed southwest. I cruised down Wilshire toward Fairfax, passing cars nicer than mine carrying people more beautiful than me.

I hated being an actor out here, where everyone is an actor. I missed New York and talking with people about things other than being in "the biz." I needed to cowboy up and buckle down. Quit bitching and get the damn job.

I got a bit twisted with the final few turns, but eventually found a spot down the street from the casting office. As I pulled into my spot with the parallel-parking virtuosity of a native Noo-Yawkah, I saw a sweet thing in a power suit rolling up with her audition pages. She passed by my car and then got in her own, and I was struck by how much she resembled the lovely film actress Samantha Mathis. I felt even less attractive. I furrowed my brow, threw on my jacket, and headed into the waiting area with the suited, sculpted masses.

I waited.

I fumed.

I waited.

"Adam Richman?"

I stood. I clenched my teeth. Quietly, under my breath, I said the little prayer that I say before every audition and performance, and I entered the room.

I tried to break the ice with a joke.

"Wow, every actor in LA broke out their lawyer suits for this, huh? The ladies, too? I even saw that Samantha Mathis look-alike coming out of the room!"

"That *was* Samantha Mathis."

"Oh."

Open mouth, insert foot.

"Why don't you start when you're ready," Eileen said.

Now, whether it was because I felt so compromised by my inadvertent diss of a certified star or because of the cumulative effect of getting my ass kicked in by LA, I got amped and angry and my game got razor sharp.

I focused, I listened, and I rocked the audition.

Rocked it.

I saw it in Eileen's face.

"You know, I saw you at your Yale showcase a year ago. You're a very good actor."

And just like that, it was like all the shit I'd endured here in LA never happened. I'm a good actor and, despite having worked pretty consistently, I now knew that someone besides Mom thinks so. I left the audition feeling powerful and as though my body-fat percentage had dropped.

My phone vibrated. I flipped it open. It was a cute British girl I'd met while doing extra work. She wanted to grab drinks at a bar in Hollywood later.

I put on my shades and swore I heard Randy Newman intone "I love LA" over the traffic. I headed to Santa Monica for lunch. Aside from a few parts of Los Feliz and Silverlake, Santa Monica is the only place I've found in LA where people seem to walk, and my fired-up New York sensibilities made me need to walk around for a bit.

And, LA be damned, I wanted carbs. I wanted to find a taste of home.

And holy shit I found it, at a slightly sad, older-looking, green-trimmed diner on Wilshire called Callahan's.

The place looked like a New York diner and was virtually empty. The booths were well worn, and I felt an instant kinship with all those who had eaten here before me, all the actors, writers, and dreamers who had slid across these ancient emerald benches and flipped through these laminated menus since the place opened in '48. After talking to the waitress, who seemed as though she may have been born there, I decided the fresh roasted turkey was the way to go. The waitress beamed with pride over the fact that they roast turkeys daily, and a quick glance at the menu revealed that they put turkey in damn near everything. It read like the post-Christmas turkey list from *A Christmas Story*: turkey salad, roasted turkey, turkey omelets, turkey sandwiches and salads, turkey soup.

THE INTERIOR OF CALLAHAN'S

I went for a diner classic, a turkey salad club, but I added a Cali twist with avocado (to me, having awesome fresh avocados is one of the best aspects of living in LA). I read the *LA Weekly* as I waited for my food, the words "You're a very good actor" still echoing in my head.

The waitress brought my food and a coffee. The sandwich was a glorious triple-decker of bacon, lettuce and tomato, and turkey salad that smelled like Thanksgiving Day, with huge chunks of meat that were perfectly juicy and not overly mayonnaised.  And there, right beside it, buttery green and chartreuse wedges of ripe California avocado. All on wheat toast with golden brown, perfectly crispy diner steak fries.

It was exactly what I needed and exactly the food manifestation of being told you're a good actor by a notable casting director. Nutty wheat toast gave way to the watery crunch of iceberg lettuce and sweet tomato, coupled with the juicy, almost gamey smokiness of fresh-roasted turkey salad, the salty crunch of the bacon, and the creamy smoothness of the avocado. Carbs, fat, salt, and nitrates—anti–Los Angeles cuisine for sure, but Lord, was I happy.

I paid my check and strolled down Wilshire, past an incredible

Did you know that avocado comes from the Nahuatl (a language of the indigenous Nahua people of Mexico) word for testicle because of its shape? Well, it does take some balls to name something delicious and edible after trouser plums!

variety of ethnic specialty shops: English, Indian, Turkish, and Russian. I looked great in my suit, my belly was overjoyed, and I'm a very good actor.

I headed home and awaited the call from my agents telling me that I would be playing the next New York lawyer from the streets with smarts but a still-streetwise edge.

I parked, hung up my suit, changed my clothes, and hit the treadmill while watching *SportsCenter*.

And I waited.

And I waited.

And I—

Flip phone rang. My agent, Susie.

I stopped running.

"So, Adam, I heard from Eileen's office."

Here it comes . . . Tell De Niro we'll do lunch next week . . .

"And they said you really rocked the piece."

"Uh-huh." I was beaming.

"And they thought you were great, but . . . "

But?!?!?!?

"They're probably going to try to go for a big name for that role. But Eileen said that you're . . . "

"A very good actor. Yeah, yeah, I know." A lump formed in my throat.

"And that she'll keep you in mind for future stuff."

"I'm sure," I said, rolling my tear-filled eyes.

"Adam, listen. It's really good when a casting director like that gives you feedback like that."

"No, it's good when they cast you, Susie."

"Adam. I'm serious. Eileen wouldn't say that if she didn't mean it."

"I'm sure, Susie," I said, with visions of hourly-wage jobs

dominating the smog-filled horizon for the next foreseeable bit of future. "I've gotta go. G'night."

I hung up the phone.

I choked back tears.

I punched a hole in the wall.

I slumped to the ground with bloody knuckles and stayed there on my knees for what seemed like hours. Silent, broken, broke, and defeated—good actor or not.

Flip phone rang.

"Richman!"

It was Geoff, one of the best, closest friends anyone in the world could hope for, one who has stood by me in good times and bad.

"I thought you were with your family in New England."

"Just home, my man. Get over here."

"Man, shit's all fucked up here."

"Man, it's LA. Shit's fucked up all over. That's why this place is so cool!"

"Oh," I deadpanned, "that's why."

"Dude, what's up with you?"

"Either I broke a mirror on a black cat under a ladder on the Ides of March, or Fate just enjoys knocking the crap out of me. I'm beat, man. I'm just tired of the struggle and always hearing 'no,' of never being good enough, of always struggling to get the next gig."

"Then quit, homes, because that's what being an actor is, man. It's a struggle, especially out here. But hey, you're a very good act—"

"Dude, can you please not say that today?"

Like so many of its residents, LA is a city that is forever in flux, and therefore why we eat what we eat in Los Angeles may have more to do with a particular moment in time than the history that came before it. Los Angeles (literally "The Angels," *not* "The City of Angels") is the second-largest city in the country, the third-largest economic center in the world, and home to more than 14 million people of exceptionally diverse ethnic backgrounds— and palates. Talking about Los Angeles's culinary identity is a task akin to hitting a moving target.

It was founded in 1781 by Spain and then became a Mexican territory when that country achieved independence from Spain. In 1848, after the Mexican-American War, it became part of the United States.

It is, of course, the hub of the entertainment industry, and people, including yours truly, come to LA by the busload, carload, and planeload to "make it." It is hard to find a "native" Angeleno since so many people here are from elsewhere, and the population is always in flux. Hobbled inextricably to the entertainment industry is an overwhelming preoccupation with appearance and health, and as diet trends come and go, restaurants in LA are forever altering their menus to keep up with the toned, tanned Joneses.

Another key factor that manifests itself on the plates of Angelenos is geography; because LA is so spread out, one must drive to live there, and drive-thrus offering quick grab-n-go foods like burgers and tacos dot the culinary landscape in the entertainment capital. This mobile food trend has now gone a step further with the proliferation throughout Los Angeles of food trucks that sell everything from grilled cheese to Korean tacos to ice cream sandwiches.

And let's not discount geology. Los Angeles sits on the Pacific Ring of Fire, the horseshoe-shaped zone of the regions of the world with the most-active volcanoes and the most-intense earthquakes.

This has had major ramifications for Los Angeles's solvency as a city—seeing as how it repeatedly gets hit with earthquakes, and scientists predict more to come—and for its soil composition, as the activity below the earth releases various compounds into the workable terrain above.

The result is nutrient-rich soil. Add to that the fact that LA has a subtropical Mediterranean climate that seldom receives more than 30 days of rainfall per year. This sunny weather creates perfect planting conditions, but sadly also brings with it the danger of drought. Plus, LA is a classic example of a microclimate system, in which the temperature can vary by nearly 20°F from city to coast. This enables the region as a whole to sustain multiple kinds of vegetation and agriculture.

Because of its subtropical climate and proximity to Central California, where 8% of the total US agricultural output originates, LA has year-round access to the kinds of fresh seasonal fruits and vegetables the rest of us wait for all year long, most notably avocados, asparagus, artichokes, figs, and dates.

This abundance of agricultural bounty has given rise to the phenomenon known as California cuisine, a style of cooking that focuses on local, fresh, and seasonal ingredients and often fuses cooking styles and ingredients from different influences or cultures. This cuisine was championed by a chef who became the culinary

Wolfgang Puck named his Chinois restaurant for the term used to describe the synthesis of Chinese and French cooking. He's also in the movie *The Muse*, playing himself, and is really creepy on film.

world's first superstar with dishes like Peking duck pizza and Chinese chicken salad: Wolfgang Puck.

So, what are the influences that have shaped California cuisine?

In 1965, the US government lifted restrictions on immigration from Asia, resulting in an incredible influx of people, foods, spices, and culinary talents and traditions from Asia—and I mean from *all over Asia*. LA's downtown boasts both Little Tokyo and Chinatown, while Wilshire Boulevard is home to Koreatown and the eastern end of Hollywood Boulevard has Thai Town.

The Asian community has influenced the LA dining landscape, and indeed the nation's, by spawning the sushi craze and popularizing *boba*—tapioca pearl milk tea. Plus, the Asian markets in each of these

Here are some cool facts about LA's Asian communities: LA contains the largest Thai population outside of Thailand; Koreatown has the largest concentration of nightclubs and 24-hour businesses and restaurants in Southern California; Little Tokyo was the birthplace of the California roll, invented by chef Ichiro Mashita at the Tokyo Kaikan sushi restaurant; and Chinatown was designed by Hollywood film set designers, and film director Cecil B. DeMille donated Chinese set pieces "from the Oscar-winning 1937 film *The Good Earth*" to add to Chinatown's atmosphere.

Five More Great Asian Districts Besides San Fran, LA, and New York

1. San Jose, California
2. Washington, DC
3. Oklahoma City, Oklahoma
4. Portland, Oregon
5. Atlanta, Georgia

neighborhoods supply hard-to-find ingredients to culinarily adventurous Angelenos looking for a taste of the East.

Now, it should go without saying that a city that was originally called El Pueblo de Nuestra Señora la Reina de los Angeles del Río de Porciúncula, that is just a short drive north from Mexico, that calls its residents Angelenos, must owe a tremendous culinary debt of gratitude to its Latino forebears.

California can claim colonial Spaniards, Mexicans, and Meso-Americans as its earliest communities, and cuisines of Mexican and Spanish origin are unquestionably the most popular in Southern California.

There are taco shops of varying quality all over Los Angeles, most of which also serve burritos, quesadillas, cemitas, chalupas, and tortas in addition to their titular dish. And because of the huge Latin population in LA, many different regions of Mexico are represented in these often-amazing mom-and-pop shops. It's not uncommon to find ultratraditional fare like the amazing hangover cure-all soup menudo, and pozole as well.

I would also be remiss should I fail to mention the countless dishes contributed by Caribbean and Central and South American Latin cultures, ranging from Salvadorian pupusas (stuffed tortillas) to Puerto Rican mofongo and Dominican fufu (both mashed, seasoned plantains with meat).

Recently, the preference for fresh, seasonal, and healthy waistline-conscious food has been making its mark on LA's Latin cuisine, too. So much so, in fact, that it's birthed a whole new style of food known as Baja-style Mexican, so-named for the southern peninsula of California that is part of Mexico. This style of Mexican cooking departs from the often heavy, cheese-laden fare that we associate with Mexican restaurants and focuses on fresh, seasonal vegetables and local, fresh-caught seafood.

So LA has constantly shifting food trends and an even more fluid populace, and everyone is on the go. People who move to LA often complain about missing seeing the seasons change, but missing out on the seasons is more than made up for by what is pretty much a culinary wonderland: The tacos are healthy; the summer fruits are evergreen; the Asian cuisine tastes as good as what you'd get in Seoul, Tokyo, and Taipei; and the foods of Mexico have safely crossed the border into our menus, fridges, and hearts. Where the decadent and delicious walk hand in hand with the healthy and heart-conscious, dodging paparazzi and potholes, eating kimchi tacos and organic couscous, riding off into the purple orange sunset as the music swells.

Roll credits.

Somehow Geoff convinced me to head over to his apartment. So, I rinsed the blood off of my hand and headed north on La Brea toward Hollywood, then east toward Geoff's place. As I crossed Western, I passed the Korean shops on the way into Little Armenia and Thai Town, near where Geoff lived on Kingsley between Hollywood and Franklin.

I saw Geoff and he gave me a bro hug. We hung out for a bit and then Geoff squirted me in the eye with a water gun. "Stop moping! It's dinnertime!"

"Dude, I gotta watch calories. I have to avoid carbs."

"Man, screw carbs and calories! You like chicken and sauce?"

"What kind of chicken? What sauce?"

"I'm taking you to Zankou," he said.

A quick drive to Normandy and Sunset brought us to Zankou Chicken, a Middle Eastern restaurant in a strip mall that specializes in roasted and rotisserie chicken. I'd never been there before, so I followed Geoff's lead. He ordered a chicken shawarma plate with extra garlic sauce. I did the same.

The lights in the restaurant were too bright, the Formica seats orange and hard. I was instantly grateful we were taking our dinners to go.

Back at Geoff's, we threw on a movie and set down our Styrofoam containers. Not since the golden glow emanating from the suitcase in *Pulp Fiction* had the opening of a box filled someone with such wonder.

There were so many flavors and foods in my box that I was mesmerized. I saw pickled veggies and small semihot peppers, creamy tahini sauce, and thicker, grainier hummus with a bit of oil and paprika. And then there was the chicken. Small chunks of alternately juicy or slightly crispy meat carved from a spinning cone of stacked chicken breast were piled high in the center of it all,

My Must-Have Bites in Los Angeles

- Chicken Shawarma— Zankou Chicken
- Crab Hand Roll— Katsuya
- Double-Double Animal Style—In-N-Out Burger
- Chicken with Mojo Sauce and rice and beans—Versailles
- Cemitas or chalupas— Taqueria Don Adrian

falling into all the sauces, soaking up all that sesame, garlicky fab-
ulousness. The garlic sauce itself was one of the wonders of the
world, served in little plastic ramekins and thicker than mayo or
sour cream, with a slightly grainy, mustardlike consistency. Off-
white and deeply fragrant with the perfume of the stinking rose, it
was creamy, garlicky perfection. My phone rang. It was the British
girl! I looked down at my chicken, realizing that it was absolutely
the worst thing to have before a date.

"Hey, luv! How're ya?"

"Good, good, I guess. Where are you? Out at that bar?"

"Nah, thought it might be too much of a faff."

"A wha'?"

"Too much of an ordeal—going out, putting on the face, you
know. Would rather just get some good food and watch a movie, to
be honest."

"Oh, I see." Sure, why wouldn't she cancel? Dammit! Would
something go right?!?!

"Interested?"

"In what?"

"Watching a movie, eating takeout?" I looked at the bedouin
bounty before me.

"Actually, I'm a step ahead of you. You have a friend?"

"What?"

"My friend and I just started a movie at his place, not too far
from you, and we've barely started eating. If you have a friend, you
should join us!" Geoff punched me in the arm.

"The kid is back!" he whispered.

"Um, yeah, I suppose I could ask my friend Charlotte. What are
you eating?"

"Geoff took me to Zankou. It's a Middle Eastern chicken place
on—"

"I know Zankou! I love that place! Give me the address and about an hour." I hung up and looked at Geoff. He tried to read the triumph and confusion on my face.

"What, dude, what?"

"We have got to clean this place up."

"What?"

"Luke! We've got company!"

Forty-five minutes later, two lovely ladies with their own Styrofoam boxes redolent of garlic were sitting on Geoff's couches and dunking pita bread in hummus right beside us. Four out-of-work actor-model-singer-writer-dancer types bonding in the shelter of deliciousness and friendship. We shared garlic sauce and common experiences and our feeling of always waiting by the phone. We fed each other; we laughed at the movie; my hand slowly began to heal.

"Adam, where are you from?" asked Charlotte.

"Brooklyn, New York."

"How has your time been in LA?"

Geoff looked at me as my lovely companion fed me a bite of chicken. "How *has* your time been in LA?" Geoff asked.

An hour ago, I would have been pissed if someone had asked me that question. But I thought about it a bit, looked down at my delicious meal and then out to the palm trees swaying outside of Geoff's window. Maybe I was drunk on some of the greatest chicken I've ever had, but I said, "LA is pretty cool. I like it here."

"The kid is back," Geoff exclaimed.

You're damn right, buddy. The kid *was* back.

And he's a very good actor.

MY GUACAMOLE RECIPE

Serves a crowd or 4 hungry dudes

Avocados to me are the edible manifestation of Nirvana, and LA is avocado heaven. The following is a version of guacamole that I make, but feel free to tweak the recipe to your own taste.

4–6 ripe Hass avocados, seeded and peeled

Juice of 3 limes

3–4 plum tomatoes, seeded and chopped

1 medium white onion, finely chopped

3–4 garlic cloves, finely minced

1 jalapeño chile pepper, seeds and ribs discarded,
    finely chopped

1 teaspoon ground cumin

1 teaspoon cayenne

Pinch of sugar

Sriracha hot sauce

Kosher salt and freshly ground black pepper, to taste

1 bunch cilantro, leaves only, well-washed, dried,
    and chopped

Mash the avocados with a fork or your hands in a bowl. Don't make it too smooth; leave some chunks. Add the lime juice and combine.

Add the remaining ingredients, stir just until combined, and serve immediately on everything in sight.

CHAPTER 2

★ ★ ★

THE *HAOLE* AND THE HOTTIE

An Adventure of Actualization and Consumption in Oahu

★ ★ ★

HONOLULU, HI

Kawela Bay

☆ **Giovanni's Shrimp Truck**

☆ **Kahuku Superette**

Pupukea ⑧③ Kahuku

Laie

Aoki's Shave Ice Waimea

Hauula

M. Matsumoto ☆☆
Grocery Store

Waialua · Haleiwa

Punaluu

Mokuleia · Kamooloa Oahu

Kaaawa

Whitmore Village

Schofield Barracks Mi
Re

Waikane

ervation

Wahiawa

ey

⑧③ Kahaluu

aha Kunia Camp Waipio Acres

H2

Waianae Ahuimanu · Heeia

ervation Waipio Kaneohe

Maili · Lualualei Pearl City Waimalu H3 Kailua

Nanakuli

Makakilo City H1 Aiea Maunawili Wa

Honouliuli

Ewa Villages ✈ **Hickam AFB** H1

Ewa

Ewa Beach ★ **Honolul**

Pearl Harbor
Naval Station

HONOLULU

"Hawaii is one of those places that keeps topping itself—just when you think you'll never see a sunset as beautiful, there comes a sunrise that even Gauguin can only imagine. It kind of makes unemployment easier to take."

—THOMAS SULLIVAN MAGNUM III, PI

I've been to Honolulu twice. The first time I had my then-girlfriend as companion, and the trip was to be the death knell of our relationship, the classic shared vacation taken too early. We did touristy things, as one is wont to do in Waikiki: saw Don Ho (who rocked, though he looked a mite rough), snorkeled Hanauma Bay, wore tuberose leis.

But the whole time we were there, all I really wanted to do was explore the islands in a roofless jeep.

I don't know why—I've never owned a jeep before and don't know how I connected it with Hawaii, but perhaps the balmy weather, volcanic peaks, and laid-back lifestyle had me yearning to roll doorless, shoeless, roofless, and carefree around our lush 50th state.

Prior to that first visit, I had done research on where to get jeeps, how much to pay, where to travel, routes to take, places to park and gas up. I had thought of everything—except my damn driver's license. Yup, this was before airport travel turned into a steaming pile of horseshit, and such things as valid state identification were not required. I could not drive—and won't bore you with the details of the lame trip my ex and I took to the Dole plantation with me riding shotgun in a Geo Prism. Suffice it to say, my craving for the experience of an excursion to the North Shore in a jeep was *not* satisfied. I wanted more. I wanted it on my terms, and I wanted it roofless, American, and vintage, with the wind in my hair, shades on my mug, and coconut on my breath.

And I would be damned if I'd let this chance pass me by again. Me. Jeep. North Shore. Minus roof. Go!

This time around, fortune had smiled on me. I was lucky enough to make the acquaintance of a woman who was entirely too foxy, and now, here I was, with time on my hands, money in my pocket, and a gorgeous woman willing to ride shotgun. All I needed was the jeep.

I found the little rental place I'd scoped out with my ex a decade earlier, and, sure enough, they had old, beat-up, badass MacArthur-era-style jeeps. Old, boxy, and non-aerodynamic. Holes in the floorboard to allow rainfall to drain out. Paint—a worn, deep burgundy wine color. Bruised, battered, and beautiful. Like life. Like me.

"Where do I sign?"

Nary a roof, nary a door, nary a moment to lose. Gorgeous woman hopped into the passenger seat through a doorless entry. I grabbed the roll bar and swung my open-shirted, board-short-wearing, flip-flopped frame into the driver's seat. Glanced heavenward and saw nothing but a vast expanse of blue. I was happy. I was hungry. And I was on a mission. Key turned, American metallic muscle growled. Let's blow this poi stand.

★ ★ ★

Oh, Hawaii.

Hawaii. Hawaii. Hawaii.

Just say it.

It's like a lullaby, a hammock swing, a sigh, a release.

Hawaii.

It sounds like a tropical birdcall, a password, an invocation of a spirit, a prayer.

Hawaii—the way your mouth boomerangs around that *w* makes you feel wistful, giddy, foreign, and far away.

Hawaii. It's awesome.

It's the place we travel to when we make a break for paradise, when we win a game show, or when we get a convenient package from our travel agent. It's the land of the shimmering sunset, adventuring spirit, slack key guitar, and nearly-English English. It is a place that we, as Americans, can call our own and yet it is so far away from anything we know. It is a plausible paradise for all of us.

When you go to Hawaii—and you will go to Hawaii, whether it's on your honeymoon or you finally come to your senses and realize that nirvana does exist and it isn't nearly as far as you think—you'll have to figure out which island to visit. There are actually more than 100, though most people go to one of the eight large islands, which include Maui, Kauai, and Hawaii (the largest of the islands, called the Big Island to distinguish it from the state itself). I'm singing the praises of Oahu, which is home to one of Hawaii's famous cities, Honolulu, and offers some incredible delights, including those off the beaten path. After all, Oahu is referred to as the Gathering Place, and Honolulu literally means "sheltered bay" or "place of shelter." How much more inviting can a getaway destination be?

Honolulu is the state capital and its Waikiki neighborhood is both the heart of Hawaii's tourist industry and its major center of commerce. Because more than 60% of visitors to Hawaii (or, in the local lingo, *haoles*, pronounced how-lees) head to Honolulu, it offers restaurants of every discipline and ethnic derivation at every price point. However, I do warn you that you'll have to apply due diligence to avoid tourist traps in your quest for the great Hawaiian eats, or, as they're known, the *ono kine grindz*.

And, interestingly, the 50th of these-a-here United States has one of the coolest culinary identities around, because it has a story—just not the one that you think you know.

Right now, close your eyes and picture a spread of Hawaiian food. What flavors do you conjure up? What dishes? What ingredients? I'll lay 10 to 1 you thought of coconuts, or maybe pineapples and ham, the two brave edible soldiers who walk hand in hand onto the menus of your local pizza joint and burger hole.

And the funny part?

Coconuts, pineapple, and pork aren't native to Hawaii, although they've come to epitomize of Hawaiian food. The fact is, Hawaii was a blank slate, historically and agriculturally speaking, before a diverse group of peoples settled there, bringing with them the foods and cultures of their homelands. Of course there were a few succulent plants and ferns, and, as with most islands, an abundance of seafood has always been within grasp. But most of the goodies that we consider Hawaiian—like the aforementioned coconuts, pineapples, and pork—were introduced by outsiders, starting with the islands' first inhabitants: the Marquesans from Polynesia.

These early Polynesian people took advantage of the island's rich volcanic soil and planted myriad varieties of root vegetables, like sweet potatoes and taros (which are famously used to make poi, the pasty, purple staple food of Hawaii).

Poi is sometimes qualified as one-finger, two-finger, or three-finger, according to the consistency of the poi and how many fingers are required to eat it, as fingers were traditionally the utensil of choice for eating poi and the looser the consistency, the more fingers you'd need to scoop it out of a bowl. Two-finger is generally the preferred consistency.

Because animal-wise the Hawaiian Islands were essentially inhabited only by reptiles and bats, the Polynesians brought with them pigs and (sorry, I know this will be hard to take) dogs both to eat and to sacrifice. Their cooking implement of choice was the *imu*, an earthen oven that was heated with hot volcanic rocks covered with two layers of leaves: one to keep the food from being scorched and to create steam and a second to impart flavor to the food. In effect, the imu steamed and roasted the food at the same time—a method called *kalua*—and one cooking session often provided food for several days.

Many people of Polynesian descent settled in Hawaii, but it remained fairly isolated until 1778. British explorer and navigator Captain James Cook landed at Waimea Harbor, Kauai, in January 1778, and everything began to change. (It bears noting, especially in a foodie book, that Cook originally named the islands the Sandwich Islands after the fourth Earl of Sandwich, his sponsor.) Captain Cook brought with him seeds for crops like melons, as well as English pigs and boars. Five years later another British captain, George Vancouver, brought cattle to Hawaii and changed it irrevocably. The lush soil provided incredible grazing fodder for the livestock, and since they—

like so many of the species introduced to the islands—had no natural predators, they began to be fruitful and multiply all over the damn place. It fell to an American named John Parker to get the cattle under control, a feat he accomplished quite effectively by butchering many of them, and, consequently, beef debuted in the Hawaiian diet.

In 1813, 20 years after beef made its arrival in paradise, a Spaniard named Don Francisco de Paula Marín planted Hawaii's first crop of pineapple. But it was not until 1901, when James Dole, the undisputed "Pineapple King," started his Hawaiian Pineapple Company in Oahu, that Hawaii truly became synonymous with the pineapple. By 1950, Dole's operation was the largest pineapple company in the world, and it had relocated to the island of Lanai (which he freakin' *purchased*!).

When I called Hawaii a blank slate, I was also referring to the significant impact that waves of immigrants of various races throughout the years had on what we now consider to be Hawaiian cuisine. Records show that Chinese immigrants, mostly Han Chinese, arrived in Hawaii as early as 1778 with Captain Cook. Their notable contributions to the Hawaiian menu were Cantonese cuisine, including such classic Chinese preparations as dim sum and stir-fries, and the substitution of rice for the traditional poi in dishes.

Japanese immigrants began to arrive in Hawaii in 1868. The first wave of about 150 people was considered illegal by the Japanese government because it resulted from a labor contract between the former Japanese government, which had just changed hands, and a broker (who was not the king of Hawaii). The first "legal" workers, sanctioned by the Japanese government and King Kalakaua (the last king of Hawaii), arrived in 1885. Most were hired as laborers for the local sugarcane and pineapple plantations. By 1920, people of Japanese descent constituted 43% of the population in Hawaii. Japanese cooks introduced *katsuo* (fried cutlets) and sashimi to the local cuisine, and they cultivated soybeans to make tofu and shoyu (soy sauce). One of the coolest aspects of the Japanese influence on the Hawaiian palate was this: Because Japanese cuisine doesn't require the use of an oven, techniques familiar to the Japanese immigrants—like frying, broiling, and simmering—became popular with other immigrant groups, who rarely had ovens in their modest homes. As a result, udon and soba noodle soups and the classic fried tempura became hugely popular in Hawaii. Plus, nori (seaweed sheets) and furikake (seasoning flakes) were integrated into many Hawaiian dishes.

The Portuguese (referred to by many in the island pidgin as Porrogee) arrived by 1899—more than 10,000 of them, in fact—also to work on the sugarcane plantations. The Portuguese immigrants' food was based in larger part on pork, and their delicious sausage became prevalent in Hawaiian cuisine. (You must try uhu, parrotfish baked in an imu with Maui onion and Portuguese sausage, it is unreal.) The Portuguese also added various chiles to the Hawaiian plate. But their most lasting contribution was pão doce, fresh-baked Portuguese sweet bread, which remains a major fave throughout the archipelago.

Tragedy brought an influx of Puerto Ricans in 1899, when their island was hit by not one but two hurricanes, leveling the sugar industry there. This made Hawaiian sugar a hot commodity and led the Hawaiian plantation owners to recruit and hire the highly skilled Puerto Rican laborers who found themselves unemployed. By October 1901, more than 5,000 Puerto Ricans had made new homes on the four main islands.

Korean immigration to Hawaii began in the early 1900s. Korean immigrants introduced the fermented spiced-cabbage awesomeness known as kimchi and, of course, their unique style of barbecuing marinated beef and pork. With the influx of rice-loving cultures and the expansion of the Hawaiian rice crop, the Korean favorite known as bibimbap (or "crazy mixed-up rice") became a major staple. Even the chile pepper flavoring pastes like duenjiang (which, I should add, is amazing in all sorts of contexts) caught on in Hawaii.

All of these different settlers—and of course we have to add Americans to the mix—greatly influenced the Hawaiian diet.

Recently there is a movement afoot to preserve Hawaii's indigenous cuisine in the face of proliferating tourist, hotel, and gimmick food. In fact, in 1992 a consortium of local chefs, including Hawaiian culinary icon Sam Choi (an eerie doppelganger for my grandpa mixed with Santa Claus), spearheaded a movement to "link local agriculture with the restaurant industry, making Hawaii Regional Cuisine a reflection of the community."

So where does one go to find all this culinary anthropology made manifest? One could go on and on about the myriad places on the leeward side of the Big Island, where the concrete canyons of Waikiki are home to every major national retailer and lei/ukelele/aloha shirt purveyor, and where fine hotels offer finer dining and back-alley cooks feed the great culinary minds the foods their aunties used to make. But the real reason that I advocate Oahu as the island you must visit is the North Shore.

Located on the windward section of the island, the North Shore is a thing of legendary beauty. It's known for its awe-inspiring,

often terrifying surf breaks and offers a
simpler way of life than that found in the
bustling commerce of Honolulu. It
stretches from Punaluu and Laie in the
east, through the legendary Sunset
Beach and the beaches of Waimea, to

Kaena Point at the extreme west. It truly will take your breath
away. It is easily one of my favorite places on planet Earth.

With the exception of a few major tourist sites like the Polynesian Cultural Center and the Turtle Bay Resort (made famous in
the film *Forgetting Sarah Marshall*), the businesses here are much
more of the cottage-industry variety, giving these communities a
small-town, unspoiled, open-minded ambience you do not find in
the city. The restaurants are generally smaller, more casual, and
cheaper. The access to true, authentic Hawaiian grub seems easier,
and because the towns are so small, you can get a different experience merely by travelling two or three miles down the Kamehameha
Highway. You can hike, surf, jump off a ridonkulously huge rock,
snorkel through reefs, and truly allow your inner adventurer to
play in a way that you simply cannot in Honolulu. When as a fourth
grader I got my 1984 *World Book Encyclopedia* and looked up
Hawaii and saw those oversaturated color photos, it was the North
Shore that I was most captivated by, and those pictures didn't come
close to doing justice to the real thing. Not that my 12-year-old self
could ever have conjured a scene as enticing as the one I found
myself in now. And I was on a mission.

We dealt with traffic for a little bit as my delectable companion and I fought our way out of Honolulu, the epicenter of Oahu's

tourist industry. My heart began to sink: I finally get my doorless, roofless jeep and here I was sitting in car exhaust and traffic that might as well be LA?

A friendly smile of reassurance and a pat on the thigh from my passenger, whose open, warm Hawaiian spirit and musical vocal cadences calmed me, reminded me to be *present*. To be aware that I was in my roofless box with someone fun, and that if I weathered this bottlenecked freeway, ahead lay the magnificence of the North Shore. Onward! Tallyho!

Calling upon my days as an Angeleno and countless memories of navigating the Brooklyn-Queens Expressway to and from LaGuardia Airport, I wove and dodged my way through the madness of Kapahulu Avenue and the H-1 highway. I finally saw some daylight as I headed north on the Pali Highway. The foliage-covered mountains and hills rose sharply to my left, making me feel like I was hurtling through space at the edge of the world—and in some ways I was. The beautiful coastline fell away in a sprawling apron of blues and greens to my right at the Pali Lookout, where I had to grab a photo of myself at the helm of my mighty metal box.

We headed northwest on the Kamehameha Highway and had gone about a mile or so when I caught a glimpse of the one culinary sight that can always intrigue me: a roadside shack with a hand-painted sign. This one read Ice-Cold Coconuts. A small, light-blue structure with a corrugated metal roof and little dolphins painted on the front, the shack was almost completely obscured by the over-

growth and festooned with pineapples and coconuts hanging off the metal roof like a necklace of frayed twine.

I pulled a U-ey and headed back.

The proprietor, a woman I'd peg to be in her 50s, would not have been out of place in the *American Gothic* painting. Congenial, warm, and look-ing not unlike an older hippie, she explained that she had chilled coconuts to drink as well as some fresh juices. Since I'd never put straw to fruit before (unless it had been hollowed out and filled with a rum drink of some sort), I opted for the coconut. I asked her how tough the process of rendering a coconut drinkable was.

"There's a lot that goes into it," she said, corkscrewing a corer into the center of a hairy coconut. "You have to pay someone to go up with spikes to pick it, and it's 40 feet up. Then you have to peel it and core it." She showed me an unpeeled "green" coconut: an oblong spheroid that looked more like a large, smooth, angular wooden football.

"Is it dangerous to harvest them?"

"Oh yeah. The last guy died," she said with a notable lack of emotion.

"He fell from 40 feet up?"

"It was dreadful. It was eight months ago. And another one, Tommy, he fell. And he fell into a roof and he has pins in his legs. It's awful, just awful . . . ," she trailed off.

I expressed my deep condolences for her loss and wished her well and a good day. Strangely, though her story had made me aware of just how much work had gone into my having a cold sip of paradise on a hot day, her frankness had set me at ease somehow.

I raised the straw to my lips and sipped. The coconut water was cold, slightly milky, and as fragrant as perfume. It had a slight grassiness that I found surprisingly refreshing. I shared the drink with my companion and onward we drove.

The coast to our right glittered and shone like a sheet of cop-per chain mail on a flat turquoise sea, and the Koolau Mountains towered over us like emerald arrowheads to our left. I kept thinking about the Hawaiian Islands' volcanic birth; the rock itself looked as though it was still in motion, erupting and reaching upward from the center of the earth.

Onward we sped, laughing, drinking from our coconut, whizzing along the eastern coast of Oahu, past the sacred grounds of red earth of the Puakea Heiau, still farther north past Punaluu and several magnificent state parks, to a town, Kahuku, at nearly the northernmost point of the island.

Close to the center of the town is the Kahuku Superette, essentially a small grocery store not unlike the bodegas I'm used to seeing in Brooklyn. But a local I know had clued me in to the fact that to be found in the very back of the rather mundane-looking and somewhat understocked store was "the best poke" in Hawaii. Poke is by far one of my favorite incarnations of raw fish—rough-cut fish, usually rubbed with sea salt and spices (traditionally used to preserve the fish) and often mixed with green onion, sesame seeds, and soy sauce. Sure enough, a stroll to the back of the store revealed a line of clear plastic bins, each with a different kind of poke, including limu (a kind of algae), shoyu (soy sauce), and even tako (octopus) poke.

There was a long line in the back—in fact, most of the customers of the Superette were there for the poke. Clearly, I was not the only one in the know. The operation was a variation on self-service. When it came time to order, you grabbed the bin of your preferred poke and handed it  to the server, who weighed it out and gave you your own container. I went for the original-style poke, a half pound of ruby-colored nuggets of gorgeous raw tuna, slivers of raw Maui onion, green onion, and sesame seeds and oil with a hint of salt and soy.

I returned to my Jeep Wrangler with my lovely companion and two pairs of chopsticks. As I opened the plastic container, the smell of sesame and fresh green onion filled my nostrils and reminded me of all the great Asian flavors I'd come to love, but the taste was beyond anything I'd experienced. The fish was so fresh, so clean, that it tasted more of the sea than of the usual ferrous minerals so often associated with tuna. The texture of the fish was supple and almost velvety, further enhanced by the slippery, smoky sesame oil. This unctuousness was offset by the crunch and sweetness of the fresh Maui onion and green onion. The chunks of fish were so plentiful and of such great quality that I kept checking the price sticker, not comprehending how one could buy so much of such a high-quality dish for just five bucks.

And on an equally delicious note, my companion let me feed her a few bites. I cannot tell you how sexy it is to feed someone you dig and watch her expression and hear her exclamations as she tastes something great. The flavor, the day, and her smile—intoxicating. Welcome to the first female-and-food-induced DUI.

No, not really.

But I will say this: Watching those I care about enjoy something I enjoy (and perhaps made) is easily one of the top reasons I love food and love to cook, and it's a big part of why I encourage others (especially single men) to cook as well.

☆　☆　☆

The sharp edges of our hunger blunted, we hopped back in the wrangler and headed back on the road. Lest you imagine us rolling down the highway in shock-absorbed comfort, I want you to experience exactly what that entailed. It wasn't just "get in the car, close the door, lock the buttons, CD picks up from where it left off, idle chat till next stop . . . " Not at all. This jeep was all geometry—a far cry from the sculpted, aerodynamic conveyances that slither along our roadways today. It was squares upon rectangles. A flying box. A rumbling beast with a grill like a marauder's smile and the aerodynamism of a fridge. This was no smooth ride, nor was it an easy one. While its engine is still considered a champion in the off-road department, the experience of driving this jeep was like conquering the island on a horse that is barely broken enough not to buck you off. Flex your right foot and the four-liter, stroke-six engine answers back with a slight shimmy and a roar that reminds you that you must actively, capital *D* drive—no two-fingers-locked-in-the-wheel coasting with this vehicle. You must hold the wheel like reins, turn it like a broken field runner, and man up on this thundering metal juggernaut as if you are taming a comet, careening around paradise like a landing force, like an explorer, like someone who captures a feeling of freedom not possible in the Lower 48. I thought of muscular rowers piloting vessels against waves off the Waimea and Ehukai beaches, early explorers traversing volcanic peaks. It felt as though to tame something wild in Hawaii, be it wave, dolphin, or machine, you must be one with it. Be at the helm, yet totally in harmony with it as you ride with ancient magisterial command—eating, riding, claiming, and conquering as you go, with the light of the fiery sun setting on the Pacific illuminating your irises and macadamia nuts crunching between your molars.

Where was I?

I was driving. Thick, emerald greenery on my left; crystalline turquoise and barely beige sand to my right; tawny, raven-haired magnificence beside me; and apparently all the luck in the world. Onward, Wrangler! Onward!

We had barely rounded the northern tip of Oahu into Kahuku

when we began to see trucks that vaguely resembled mail delivery vans—doorless and boxy—advertising fresh white shrimp. Places

with names like Fumi's Kahuku Shrimp, Romy's Kahuku Prawns and Shrimp Hut, Opal Thai Food, and Giovanni's Aloha Shrimp, all boasting of their "authentic Kahuku" delicacies. In my experience, when choosing from multiple vendors of the same product and in doubt, you should always go with the oldest. And in Kahuku, the original, granddaddy shrimp truck is Giovanni's.

Giovanni's signage was old and somewhat crappy: a white wooden sign with stenciled letters under a patina of graffiti was all that denoted its existence at the side of the Kam Highway. That, to me, is a good omen. When I turned into the parking lot, we were greeted by the sight of an equally graffiti-covered truck with a menu printed on its side and picnic tables with a broad sheet of aged canvas stretched above them.

The menu advertised just five items: Scampi Shrimp, Hot and Spicy Shrimp ("no refunds"), Lemon Butter Shrimp, Garlic Hot Dog, and Extra Rice. Yes, extra rice was a menu item. I went with the classic scampi I'd heard raves about, and my

companion selected Hot and Spicy, which nearly prompted a proposal from me on the spot. After 10 minutes or so we were rewarded with two of the loveliest plates I've ever seen. Mine was a half-moon of *perfectly* cooked, tail-on, fat, gorgeous shrimp with browned garlic bits on their orange sides, two scoops of *perfectly* cooked white rice dotted with more of the aforementioned garlic bits, and a slice of lemon between the two. My friend's Hot and Spicy was the same sans garlic, but the shrimp were smothered in a slightly chunky, bright autumnal red and orange sauce flecked with chile seeds.

My, oh my, the taste.

My buttery shrimp popped and crunched as perfect shrimp do, with the smoky crunch of the redolent browned garlic throughout. My friend's Hot and Spicy was exactly that: Hot. And spicy. But as someone who is a fan of the spicy morsel, I have to say that the good people at Giovanni's achieved that culinary nirvana that is the proper balance between heat and flavor. Mixing our sauce into the rice on our plates only heightened the velvety indulgence of the dish—almost like a risotto, only not nearly as expensive and hifalutin.

And even cooler was that this time, she fed me.

We walked—full, happy, tan, and glowing—to the mighty jeep, swung ourselves in, looked at one another, and smiled.

In that moment, in ocher eyes so unlike mine, I could not discern her iris from her pupil, nor my own tendency toward romantic drama from the tectonic shift I felt in my gut when her eyes met mine. And then she said:

"I want something sweet."

I had my "Oh no she didn't!" moment, giggling in the least attractive way possible before composing myself enough to ask what she meant.

"You ever have shave ice?"

"There are the old Latino men in Brooklyn with the big ice cube, the metal shaver, and bottles of Day-Glo sugar flavoring. Like those?"

"No," she laughed. "No, Adam, not those. *Hawaiian* shave ice." Ahhh, I had heard of a place called Matsumoto's that specialized in this treat of near-snowlike powder, mixed with distinctly Polynesian flavors like the Chinese plum called li hing mui in addition to the more mundane cherry and oftentimes mixed with ice cream as well.

"Where do we go?"

"Haleiwa."

Haleiwa is a town on the Anahulu River in the Waialua District of Oahu, sometimes a teeming hub of tourist activity, sometimes as mellow and sleepy as a whaling town in Nova Scotia.

We passed the iconic Haleiwa sign with the surfer shooting a tube as we crossed the Rainbow Bridge on our way into old Haleiwa Town.

While deceptively quaint upon entry, the bustle of Haleiwa that day was nearly palpable, like the hum of an approaching swarm of bees. We heard a percussive report like the thundering of a cavalry battalion, and, lo and behold, upon rounding a curve into this small hamlet of 2,200 souls, we came upon a Japanese taiko drum performance. Despite the young age of the performers (I believe it was an Asian cultural youth society performance), the troupe was awash in color and emotion, forging an almost ecstatic level of connection between performer and audience.

Passing shave ice purveyor Matsumoto (the M. Matsumoto Grocery Store, to be specific), we were aghast to see a line that rivaled that of the downtown Brooklyn DMV branch (which I'm convinced is a circle of Hell). Luckily, a cool couple I had met in the town of Laie, around the island to the east, had clued me in that Aoki's, just down the road, was as good as if not better than Matsumoto's and would probably have a shorter line.

We pulled in next to Aoki's, a wooden store painted barn red with a corrugated metal awning. The line was indeed shorter than

at Matsumoto's, and more locals, surfers, kids, and people speaking pidgin were numbered among its occupants.

As my acquaintances had recommended, I ordered my ice with macadamia ice cream at the bottom, choosing coconut and tiger's blood flavor (some fruity mixture—no actual tigers were harmed in the making of this dessert). They placed my cone and my lovely companion's in a holder. I bought a pound of Kona coffee for my mom, and we walked to the parking lot, where everyone was eating sitting in, on, or near their cars.

The ice was feather soft and melted on my tongue like a fat snowflake. The syrups were intense bursts of flavor, but the creaminess of the ice cream cut the sharp, sugary bite and gave each bite the consistency of a Creamsicle.

A glance at the sky told us sunset was near. "We should head back," she said. A lump formed in my throat. "It's gonna get dark soon, we should get back to Waikiki."

Yup. We'd eaten at the Shrimp Truck of Knowledge, tasted the Poke of Experience and the Shave Ice of Intuition, and been cast out of Eden into the melee of commerce, buffets, and shopping of the island's leeward side.

We threw our empty ice cones away and jumped in a hunk of old metal that suddenly felt leaden and unwieldy. The Wrangler shuddered as I turned the key, and I tried to shake off the inevitable disappointment of ending this day. I looked one last time through my roofless roof at the sky, now a dusky gray-blue, and gave a resigned sigh.

And then she kissed me.

I don't know if it was the surf I heard or my own blood pounding in my ears, but . . .

"Come on, New York. We have no roof and if it rains . . . "

"It rains."

Let it come down! Let it pour!

"Let's go."

I threw the awkward gearshift into drive, stepped on the fat, flat black pedal, and snaked out into traffic, jaw clenched as grimly as Sergeant Rock of Easy Company's always was. I was a man, dammit. In paradise, at the edge of the world, on the crest of the scimitar of Polynesia. I bared my chest to the sun! I drove beautiful, brawny battering rams! I ate the fruit of the trees and the surf, and I knew the touch of beauty and bounty. A modern man in a place that felt like creation happened last week. I navigated your mountain roads! I snorkeled your reefs; I ate your pork and Spam and that pasty, purple poi. I am in love with you, Hawaii. I am in love with the volcanic surge of emotion I feel inside my chest when I'm there. I love the limitlessness of mind that your simplest vista and subtlest breeze can engender, I . . .

"I like you, New York."

I wanted to say something clever. To have my Han Solo moment and say, "I know." I wanted to meet her warmth with warmth of my own. But I knew better than to push. Instead, I smiled, nodded, and squeezed her soft, caramel hand.

"Thank you for today," she said. I looked past her at a sky peeled directly off the ceiling of the Sistine Chapel—roiling swirls of gold, azure, yellows, and whites. "Thank *you* for today," I shouted to the sky, to my creator, to her, to everyone. I smiled, then I laughed till I cried as she looked at me—amused at my amazement, at my rapture. What can I say? Happiness is addictive.

41

We rumbled our way southward on the H-2 freeway as the sky darkened around us. By the time we reached Pearl Harbor, the sky was a deep indigo. And as a bathtub-warm breeze washed over me, as her hair whipped against my cheek, I realized that though the day was over, the beautiful Hawaiian night was just beginning.

We wove through the urban grid of Honolulu, and we returned the jeep to its rightful owners. I walked round the front and tenderly rested my hand on the hood and nodded somberly, like a jockey with his Thoroughbred. If I'd had a carrot in my pocket, I would have fed the damn thing.

Good job, girl.

"Come," my friend said, waking me from my little moment, smiling, her hand extended.

I smiled back and, for a second, I thought the jeep did, too.

"Come."

I slid my hand into hers, and I swear I can still feel it today if I think about it.

I feel it all.

Oahu is still evolving, but she will always open her arms to you, whether you're eating haute cuisine in the south or shaved ice out of a plastic cone in the north. It is a plateful of immigration with a side of agriculture dunked in a hearty bowl of history.

And fortunately for us all, it's only part of the eight-part, volcanic, smoldering, succulent, salty, sweet, and macadamia-nutty story that is Hawaii.

I can hear the roar of my straight-6, the rush of the surf, the sizzle of truck shrimp, and the clipped cadences of pidgin English in my ears. Until I am back, with wind in my hair and unspoiled creation in my view, until I am back in Hawaii, I will remain in her thrall and I will never feel as good, as capable, and as strong as I do when I am in her embrace.

A hui hou.

Till we meet again.

Aloha.

AHI POKE RECIPE

Makes 4 servings

While exquisitely fresh tuna can be hard to come by outside of Hawaii, and extreme caution should be exercised anytime you eat or prepare raw foods (and while any poke I can make will suck when compared to the Kahuku Superette's), I urge you to give this basic recipe for delicious and refreshing Ahi Poke a try. It comes from a friend's mom who lives in the Kalihi neighborhood of Honolulu. In the spirit of the islands, all measurements are approximate and can be altered according to taste or availability.

> 12 ounces sashimi-grade ahi (yellowfin tuna), diced
>
> Hawaiian pink salt (or sea salt) and pepper, to taste
>
> ½ cup minced Maui onion or red onion
>
> ¼–½ cup minced green onions (green part only)
>
> ¾ cup soy sauce
>
> 2 tablespoons Asian sesame oil
>
> Sesame seeds

Place the tuna in a bowl and sprinkle with the salt. Toss gently until all of the fish is seasoned.

Add the remaining ingredients, toss again to combine, then cover and chill in the refrigerator for at least an hour and up to 4 hours.

Serve on wonton crackers, rice crackers, or simply as is.

CHAPTER 3

☆ ☆ ☆

GREETINGS FROM PLANET BROOKLYN

Or: Girls, Grits, and Growing Up in the County of Kings

☆ ☆ ☆

BROOKLYN, NY

☆ **Sahadi's Specialty and Fine Foods**

☆ **Lucali Brick Oven**

☆ **Franny's**

☆ **Pino's La Forchetta Pizzeria**

Upper New York Bay

BROOKLYN

☆ **L & B Spumoni Gardens**

Lower New York Bay

☆ **Totonno's Pizzeria Napolitano**

Breakfast is the most important meal of the day, and never is this maxim more true than after a long evening of drinking. So when I walked out into the night after a friend's insanely good and insanely insane birthday party at a hidden loft in Gowanus (which featured go-go dancers, tattoo artists, and a full bar), I stepped into the newly chic industrial area with just one thing in mind: a late-night feast. As I pondered my choices, good fortune struck in the form of a young lady from the United Kingdom who happened to be leaving the party at the same time. We exchanged some flirtatious words, and before long we were walking arm in arm through the maze of brick buildings that make up the Gowanus neighborhood along the sludgy canal of the same name.

We wandered toward Fifth Avenue, a main thoroughfare that cuts through Park Slope, Sunset Park, and (after merging with Fourth Avenue in the Bay Ridge neighborhood) all the way south to the water at the foot of the Verrazano-Narrows Bridge. The businesses were mostly closed along Fifth, but a few had begun to open their doors, and a few, like the one to which we were headed, mercifully never close. This magical place is not unique in the world, but it is as much a part of New York and Brooklyn as the subway, an indiscriminate hatred of the Red Sox, and the ability to throw the word "fuck" into almost every fucking sentence. Most people come to New York and go to a deli, a pizzeria, or a pushcart for a pretzel or dirty-water dog. Those are all quintessential New York food experiences, but the one I wish more people made a part of their trips is a diner.

My new friend and I fell giddily into a booth, dressed far too nicely for a diner, too loud and too amorous to be out in public, and too hungry for words.

We cracked open laminated menus the size of life rafts and began to scroll through the myriad choices of foods, comfort and otherwise. See, the best part about going to a diner is that they serve pretty much everything, all the time. While some diners have a distinct Greek bent, most of the dishes are straight-ahead American food. The Hellenic influence can be found primarily in the names of the places themselves (like Acropolis or Minerva), the décor (murals, columns), and even in the Greek key design of their iconic "We are happy to serve you" blue and white to-go coffee cups, as well as the odd gyro or souvlaki plate.

The late-night presence of post-revel partiers is nothing out of the ordinary for diner waitstaff. In many cases, it's (if you'll pardon the pun) their bread and butter. So we felt right at home.

As I said, the hottie in the short silk dress and killer heels who was good enough to be my companion as night gave way to early morning was a recent transplant to New York from England. For her, drunk eats meant aluminum trays of curries, kebabs, or greasy fish and chips. While I can acknowledge the post-bacchanalia mer-

While the Greek influence on diners isn't unique to New York, it did originate in the area. From the 1950s through the 1970s, Greek immigrants established more than 600 diners in and around New York, pulling off a virtual coup d'état in the very American phenomenon of prefabricated restaurants. Greeks and diners have been intertwined ever since, which is probably why you'll find Greek dishes on these everything-and-anything menus.

its of these dishes firsthand (I lived in Ireland briefly after college), nothing compares to a diner in terms of variety, level of quality, and consistency—or the ability to get breakfast 24 hours a day.

When it's drunk diner time and you need the cure-all food that's good for what ails ya, you'd be hard-pressed to find anything better than the diner breakfast. It'll have the right amount of grease, will always be tasty, and will usually be dirt-freakin' cheap.

That said, the diner can be a wee-bit overwhelming to the Weetabix set. But even a Brit can find comfort in a diner. This young lassie was new to the diner world, and because the menu—like those at just about every other diner in New York—was nearly 1,000 pages long (no, not really) plus laminated special-of-the-day inserts, she looked to me for recommendations.

I went for two eggs over-medium, wheat toast, turkey sausage, and french fries (instead of the home fries that are usually served with breakfast), plus coffee, fresh squeezed OJ, and a *large* glass of much-needed ice water. I ordered my meal with the fluid mellifluousness of someone who has been reciting it by rote since birth; as a Brooklyn native and diner veteran, I pretty much have.

"Wow. You're like an expert. That was skilled."

"Oh girl, you ain't seen nothing yet." Smooth, no?

"What should I get?"

"I say go with breakfast. Simple, easy, and fast."

"I hope you don't think those adjectives apply to me," she said with that unendurably foxy accent.

"No, no, no," I said, "nothing about you is simple."

She smiled and playfully threw a plastic half-and-half container at me. She ordered an egg-white omelet with goat cheese and spinach (yes, goat cheese at an all-night eatery! I love New York).

The waitress asked her what side she'd like: potatoes or grits.

"Or what?"

"Grits," the waitress repeated.

"Whassat?"

"Essentially, corn porridge," I explained, hoping that my use of the word "porridge" would both explain the dish, make her feel at ease, and earn me points on the Anglophile angle.

"Is it healthy?"

"What? Grits?"

"Is that spelled with a *z*?"

"No. G-r-i-t-s. It's hominy that's ground . . . oh, look forget it. It's really like porridge, but creamier in many ways."

"But healthy?"

"We've been partying all night and have yet to sleep, and you're really worried about *healthy*?"

"Point taken."

Grits were ordered and silly political conversation ensued. I say "silly" because I find that many political conversations are just people regurgitating what they've heard a pundit or newsperson say, and my companion's observations were no exception to that rule. Coupled with the fact that this discourse was emanating from a brand-new New Yorker who, though deeply easy on the eyes, was having a hard time controlling the volume of her voice, not unlike a newly thawed Austin Powers, I soon began to get annoyed. I chafed at her high-handed views of the American political system and her pronunciation of our first African American president's name as "Owbahmmer." In fact, were it not for the arrival of the perfectly cooked eggs, golden brown fries, crispy but not greasy turkey sausage, and nutty, buttery wheat toast, I might have gotten up to leave. With a meal so good in front of me, though, I figured I'd rather make love than war. As I searched for a joke to put a cork in her litany, I focused on my food, weathered the storm, and waited for a break in the stream of words. Before I could interrupt her, the food beat me to it.

Moaning rapturously, she gestured to the grits and then to an adorable chipmunklike mound in her cheek.

"Grits are *brilliant*!"

"Don't know if that's the adjective that I or anyone who's ever eaten grits would ever use, but I guess they are kinda brilliant."

"I mean, they use just gobs of butter, which would make anything taste yum, but the texture is just *lovely*!"

"Again, 'lovely' is not an adjective that you usually hear applied to grits."

"What adjectives does one hear?"

"'Good.' Or 'bad.'"

"Uh-huh. And these are?" I tasted them: buttery as a tin of Danish cookies, creamy as rice pudding with little pearls of hominy goodness, with a strong background flavor of salt and black pepper.

"These are 'good.' Good grits."

"'Good' seems hardly enough." Hearing her rhapsodize about grits just minutes after condemning our bicameral legislature made me laugh.

"Well, our government may be flawed, but at least we can claim success with our grits." She smiled and took the hint. I liked her even more for this.

We ate ravenously for a bit, with little snippets of small talk mixing in with perfectly runny yolks soaked up with toast; crispy, salty fries dunked into said yolks; tangy hot sauce on everything from crispy brown turkey sausage to creamy bites of egg and goat cheese.

"Look, I don't want you to think ill of me. I know I can come on a bit strong with the political stuff. What political stuff gets you?"

"Political conversations?"

"Pardon?"

"Political conversations. They make situations suck in most cases."

"So, you're saying that this situation," she said while gesturing in a circle encompassing the two of us and our loaded wood-grain Formica table, bathed in the blue half-light of the Brooklyn dawn, "this situation sucks?"

"I'm saying that with the perfection of a good night, a great party, warm weather, you across the table from me, your dimples, your accent, and these eggs right here, scathing indictments and deep analysis of government just becomes the turd in the punch bowl."

"*The what?*"

"An expression. It just means an unpleasant element in an otherwise enjoyable time."

A pause.

"So, no politics."

"Nope."

A pause.

"You like my dimples?"

"Yup."

"It's late," she said, scooping up some egg and cheese with a piece of toast.

"It's early," I said, knocking back the last swallow of my dark, oily, rich coffee and smiling at her over the rim.

"Maybe I should get a cab home?"

"Maybe."

"Maybe I shouldn't?"

"Maybe."

"Oh, I see. So, maybe I should stay and go home in a few hours?"

"Maybe you should."

And maybe she did.

And maybe she didn't.

And maybe my mom and dad taught me better than to kiss and tell.

But an early morning of diner deliciousness and an Anglo angel on a dusky Brooklyn morning will forever live in my heart.

★★★

There are two fundamental facts any reader of this book should know about Brooklyn. First, nearly one-third of all citizens in the United States can trace their roots back to Brooklyn, a fact that's not so surprising when you consider how many of the people who passed through Ellis Island (including my ancestors) settled there. Contrary to popular belief, I was not born in Brooklyn. I was actually born in Manhattan, but moved to Brooklyn because of better real estate prices and because my mom and her breast milk were there. (Dear reader: This will be the one and only reference to Mom's boobs.) Nonetheless, Brooklyn is my hometown, my heartbeat, my lifeblood, my residence, and, to me, the greatest spot in the world.

Second, there is no one cuisine that is truly emblematic of Brooklyn. That's right, I said it. There is no such thing as Brooklyn cuisine. It does, however, have on offer a more incredible variety of authentic ethnic and cultural cuisines than any other place on the planet. Because of the availability of affordable (as compared to other boroughs of New York City) housing, a significant manufacturing sector in decades past, and the original immigration settlement patterns, Brooklyn had and still has pockets of authentic, undiluted ethnic culture. There are Italian neighborhoods like Bensonhurst with food that could be straight from Palermo; Chinese neighborhoods like Sunset Park and Homecrest where the menus are written only in Chinese characters; Russian neighborhoods like Brighton Beach, where caviar and smoked fish are plentiful; and Polish neighborhoods like Greenpoint, where even my grandma would say that the brown bread and kapusta are just like they made in the Old Country. There are Irish neighborhoods, Orthodox Jewish neighborhoods, West Indian neighborhoods, Scandinavian neighborhoods, Middle Eastern neighborhoods, and many more. What's great about these enclaves is that because they are populated by first-generation immigrants for whom the per capita income can be pretty nominal, their restaurants, often run by first-generation immigrants as well, are a pretty freakin' cheap way to get an authentic taste of a faraway land. The signs are in a foreign language, the clientele and employees speak a foreign language, and the flavors are unlike anything you're used to. It's a completely immersive experience such as one you might have miles away from the United States, yet it's all to be had for the price of subway fare or a cab ride.

When I was young, a stroll along Avenue U took me from Italy to Israel to Russia to China to Ireland and back to Italy again. Because of this, we Brooklyn residents grow up "a li'l of everything." Some of my childhood friends were from Trinidad, Cuba, Israel, China, Ghana, and Poland, and when I say they were "from" there, I mean exactly that: They'd come over as small children or babies, and their folks spoke very halting English, if any. Some of the finest "ethnic" cuisine I have ever had has been eaten at the tables of my friends' families. They served dishes that they held in their hearts, under their kufis or babushkas, all the way across the

Atlantic, Pacific, Sahara, or steppes to Flatbush, Bay Ridge, or Borough Park.

I still remember my mother's co-worker Anne-Marie teaching me to run the lemon rind over the lip of my espresso cup before twisting it like a ribbon above the dark brew and tossing it in. I still remember my father's friend Peter, an Asia-born Chinese man who owned the incredible, now-defunct Chinese restaurant Ping Fong, teaching me to roll a kumquat between my fingers before eating it skin and all. This is the culinary education that a Brooklyn kid gets outside of a classroom, cookbook, or kitchen. Equally well versed in dim sum as he is in deli, your average Brooklynite is able to order a callaloo Jamaican pattie with as much confidence and aplomb as he does mozzarella en carozzo or matzoh balls.

These days, Brooklyn is considered "cool," though to we who've called it home since the Internet was a mere twinkle in Al Gore's stoic eye, this is nothing new. The awesome old-school Brooklyn that had the Brooklyn Dodgers and actual trolleys to dodge defined cool in the day when Coney Island was a shiny, new destination filled with wonder. Nathan's was new. And soda fountains selling egg creams made with Fox's U-Bet syrup and "two-cents plain" seltzer were ubiquitous. But between then and now, things were decidedly less cool in the 718. To paraphrase my childhood friend Mike, it was a different Brooklyn when we were growing up.

Now there's this other version of Brooklyn, where MTV wants to film *The Real World* and movie stars want to live; where British sports and pop stars conceive their children and name them after it (Thanks, Beckhams. You're welcome over for rice and beans anytime!); where major musical bands relocate (like Bowie did to Berlin prior to releasing *Low)* in search of artistic inspiration; where the girls are pretty and the guys are bearded and bike riding; and, where the grocery bags are canvas and the streets are littered with boutique paper shops and the Gowanus Canal runs thick with organic chai.

I grew up in Brooklyn between those two periods, a time when it was rougher, cheaper, and less polished. From the '70s to the '90s, Brooklyn was a place you lived in and you made the best of it, where you needed to "protect ya neck." You were not regarded as cool, but as hard. Here, Jewish kids and black kids alike could scream the words of "No Sleep till Brooklyn" and understand the defiant label of badass inherent in that statement as residents of "the BK." Back then, the only people who lived in Greenpoint were fresh-off-the-boat Polish people and the manufacturing employees who worked there. The gentrified area I live in now was somewhere you could see drunken Dominican men brandishing pool cues in the middle of the street at 2:00 pm. Where some of your favorite hip-hop stars dated girls in your homeroom class (true story in my case). Where hip-hop itself was emerging, evolving, and becoming the vital new voice for all straphangers, park slangers, and playground ballers.

Brooklyn was wild, wooly, raw, and *real*. You wore your identity as a Brooklyn resident like a bulletproof vest—and sometimes you wore one of those, too. Neighborhoods of cultural aspect were not considered "cute" or "destinations," they were enclaves, footholds, keeps on the borderlands between Polish, Italian, Irish, Lubavitch, and West Indian.

Things are different now.

The downtown portion of Fourth Avenue, near the banks of the sludge-ridden Gowanus Canal, historically was an ugly thorough-fare littered with auto repair shops and lumber warehouses—at least during my upbringing—but now it is home to gourmet ramen restaurants, Australian restaurants, gourmet Mexican restaurants, indie film and music venues, some great brewpubs, cafés, and a kitchen where yours truly was once the chef, making sandwiches of fig jam and watercress in a building that formerly housed a bail bondsman. No doubt that place thrived in its heyday due to the business generated by the nearby and now-defunct Brooklyn House of Detention, made famous by the Beastie Boys on *Paul's Boutique* (which, FYI, does not exist). Brooklyn is cool, cleaner for sure, and gentrified. It's hip, hot, and user-friendly. I'm prouder than ever to have lived here before it became so—and happier than ever to live here still. (We'll see if I still feel this way if the vile land grab known as Atlantic Yards comes to fruition and an ugly megastadium behemoth is built a literal stone's throw from my home.)

It also bears noting that while New York State itself has a pretty fair agricultural output, most of it originating upstate or on Long Island, no single prevailing crop determines why we eat what we eat in Brooklyn as it does in other cities I've visited. With so many ports, trains, and way stations nearby, the taste of Brooklyn is a taste of *everywhere*, condensed, undiluted, and authentic.

Which leads me to the one contradiction to this authenticity in Brooklyn's current food identity, one directly related to an entity drawn here by the promise of relatively affordable lofts, the aura of counterculture cool, and a desire to be with like-minded, fashionable culture vultures. That entity is the hipster.

This entity brings with it spending money and the cachet of cool, and a slew of great restaurants, bars, and clubs usually follows in its wake. Unfortunately, it's largely comprised of skinny douche bags in skinnier jeans with ironic facial hair, cardigans, vintage Bowie T-shirts, and half-Asian girlfriends named Chloe who work as graphic designers and wear terry cloth dresses to underground music shows in basement venues in Williamsburg.

Much of hipster culture is youth based. This means two things: The first is that Mommy and Daddy have probably provided some funds with which to taste a bit of the Big Apple, and the second is that the parents themselves need someplace to eat when they visit. Since trust-fund babies don't eat Top Ramen and their benefactors don't eat from street carts, this means that some unusually high-end places have opened throughout the borough in the past half decade.

Most of these hipster communities are very easily accessed from Manhattan, where the majority of visitors to New York City tend to stay, making some of the best food to be found in Brooklyn just a short cab or subway ride away.

The other thing is that hipster communities are generally the stomping grounds of fresh-out-of-college, got-my-first-big-boy-job-in-the-city kids (Williamsburg is known as Baby's First Manhattan). Most are situated right over the river from Manhattan in downtown (northern) Brooklyn, as in the cases of Williamsburg, Fort Greene, Prospect Heights, and, to a lesser degree, Red Hook, Greenpoint, and North Park Slope. This gives the Conversed, corduroyed masses access to Manhattan for their jobs in the research library at *Rolling Stone* or writing grant proposals for an NGO that specializes in Tibetan splinter removal. These transplants choose to live close to the subway lines, the arteries of the beating heart of New York's youth culture and workforce. All along those arteries there are now restaurants where their colleagues from Manhattan can dine when they want to feel all "downtowny" and "urbany" and that give the natives access to haute cuisine, pad thai, and excellent sushi for those nights when the cute girl from the American Apparel ad with a name that sounds like a Norwegian granola company agrees to grab dinner before the Japanther show at the Music Hall of Williamsburg ("How are you liking your sea bass, Kashi?").

In Brooklyn, property costs and rents are lower than those in Manhattan (though not by much), and accordingly, younger restaurateurs have an incentive to open their visionary eateries in the county of Kings. In some cases, like at the Cobble Hill stalwart Saul, chefs who worked below marquee chefs at mighty Manhattan establishments like Le Bernardin come to Brooklyn to live out their dreams of heading their own kitchens. And so, many upscale restaurants, with food but not prices on par with some of Manhattan's best, have sprung up in these newly gentrified neighborhoods.

★★★

With nearly 2.5 million residents, Brooklyn is New York City's most populous borough, and if it were its own city (as it was until 1898), it would be second only to Manhattan as the most densely populated city in the country. It is the "Home to Everyone from Everywhere!" as a sign off the Belt Parkway declares. And indeed it is filled with people from everywhere who have influenced Brooklyn's food identity as profoundly as lobstermen in Portland, Maine, and Mexicans in Austin, Texas. In Brooklyn, the melting pot that is this great country can truly be enjoyed on the plate—all of the different cultures, most within walking distance of each other, and nearly every cuisine represented in some delicious way. There is an endless array of places to go and things to eat, from the South American food carts at the Red Hook Ball Fields to fine-dining restaurants that rival those of any other city.

When you go to Brooklyn—and you absolutely must—you can experience all of this. But you should seek out the real Brooklyn, the one that still remains from when I was a kid and even before that. You need to have an Italian hero, a slice at a pizza

> **Great Pizza Places in Brooklyn That Aren't Too Trendy Yet**
> 1. Pino's La Forchetta—Park Slope
> 2. Franny's—Prospect Heights
> 3. Lucali—Carroll Gardens
> 4. Totonno's—Coney Island
> 5. L & B Spumoni Gardens— Gravesend

joint, and a meal at one of the many ethnic places that seem to transport you to another continent. Most of all, just relax and enjoy the *realness* (as rapper and Brooklyn-native Redman would say).

★ ★ ★

It doesn't get much realer than the mile-long extravaganza of food, culture, and general high-spirited Brooklyn-ness known as the Atlantic Antic annual street fair.

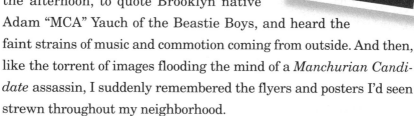

One recent Sunday I woke up late in the afternoon, to quote Brooklyn native Adam "MCA" Yauch of the Beastie Boys, and heard the faint strains of music and commotion coming from outside. And then, like the torrent of images flooding the mind of a *Manchurian Candidate* assassin, I suddenly remembered the flyers and posters I'd seen strewn throughout my neighborhood.

"The Antic!" I shouted like an ass to nobody in particular. The Atlantic Antic, held on the second weekend of September on a main thoroughfare in northern Brooklyn, is a street fair that showcases the businesses that line the street itself, promotes awareness of civic causes (Take Your Man to the Doctor Week, voter registration, sign-ups for and against key issues affecting the borough, and so on), and creates a venue for some of the best food that the city has to offer. You can get tasty stuff from the Middle Eastern shops and restaurants that line Atlantic Avenue and from the gourmet and savory places that lie on the tributary streets of the affluent Cobble Hill neighborhood to the south and the well-to-do Brooklyn Heights to the north—all of this bordered by the somewhat chaotic grid of streets around Schermerhorn and public housing, like Wyckoff Gardens, where you'd be foolish to linger too long.

Barbecue, zeppolis, falafel, burgers, and chicken roti are all represented at the Antic. There are few better ways to take a big bite of Brooklyn than spending a day at the Antic.

I hit the streets ready for the savory goodness of Brooklyn street fair food, browsing booths hawking "mozzarepas," an unholy, cheese-filled union between mozzarella cheese and an arepa (corn cake); fried Oreos (better than they sound); and Philly cheese steaks (we're not in Philly, so they're phucking phake) until I finally came upon a cart selling one of my all-time-favorite fair foods: Italian sausage and peppers.

There are many, many carts at the fair, and to the novice, their products all look the same, but I have walked a mile ahead of ye, young sausage initiates, and I shall guide you in the ways of the link. If the signage is too flash and too polished, move on; those guys are more interested in attracting a large volume of customers than they are in the food. If it sells more than just sausage and peppers, move on; Italians in the know take pride in the meats they serve, and if it's a "sausage and pepper" cart, that should be all it serves. If it does not offer a choice between "sweet

61

and mild" or "hot" sausage, move on; every good salumeria (Italian pork store) carries both, and every good vendor does too.

I walked over to a reasonably busy cart (always a good sign), and there, laid out on the cast-iron flattop grill like a bone Native American breastplate or meaty rows of matching parentheses, were fat sweet and hot Italian sausages browning next to one another. The sausages were shiny with grill oil and their own fat. Alongside this meaty armada was a softened, oily mass of red and green bell peppers and onions that were cooked to the point of translucence. The cart exuded a fragrance somehow melding backyard cookout, pizzeria, and the sweet-smokiness of caramelized veggies.

I did as I usually do and ordered the hot sausage, as I consider the sweetness of the onions a great counterpoint to the red pepper flakes in the sausage. (Plus, I'm sweet enough—ba-dum-pum.) I asked for the sausage to be well done too, because when charred, the natural casings have a great, chewy, almost decadent juicy pop when you bite into them. The sweet, very tiny but loud lady who took my money grabbed a crusty length of Italian bread and loaded it with one of the brick red seven-inch sausages. Using one side of her tongs as a spoon, she scooped up some Technicolor, mushy wonderfulness of peppers and onions and laid an inch-thick layer of them atop the sausage. She wrapped it in waxed paper, gestured me in the direction of the condiments, and shot me a quick nod that seemed to say, "You're good? Great, now move the fuck down so I can feed the next guy."

A squirt of hot mustard and I was ready to perch on the bumper of a parked car and dig in. The smell was a rich, almost perfumey blend of oil, grilled meat, and pepper, and the first bite was utterly

Great Condiments You Probably Don't Have
in Your House, but Should

- Huy Fong sriracha Asian pepper sauce (green top and rooster on the front)
- Kewpie Japanese mayo
- Ssamjang (Korean fermented soybean paste—amazing)
- Gochujang (Korean red chile paste)
- Chipotle chiles (whole in adobo sauce or as a paste)
- Heinz HP sauce (British all-purpose condiment)
- Yellow miso paste
- Shichimi togarashi (Japanese seven-spice blend)
- Recaito or sofrito (major Puerto Rican flavors)
- Sazon (Latin spice blend)
- Tomato pickle (available at Indian markets)
- Mango chutney
- Fig jam
- Pickapeppa sauce (Jamaican flavoring)
- Taramasalata (Greek caviar spread)
- Giardineria (Italian pickled vegetables)
- Chowchow (pickled vegetable relish)
- Ajvar (Turkish red bell pepper spread)
- Crème fraîche (like sour cream on steroids)

orgasmic. The fresh bread had a bit of a crunch that yielded to a toothy tear. The mustard and the unctuous vegetable mixture hit the roof of my mouth as my tongue and lower jaw cut through the spicy richness of the sausage, which gave way with an incredible, crispy snap.

I finished my sandwich, bought a delicious Brooklyn-brewed Sixpoint ale, and walked on toward the East River end of Atlantic Avenue.

As I strolled, I watched high schoolers perform dance routines and capoeira practitioners in a fighting circle do a demo, listened to our colorful borough prez speak about boroughwide concerns, and soaked it all in. As I neared a friend's home, where I hoped to hang for a bit, I ducked into the amazing Middle Eastern provisions store called Sahadi's for some goodies to take home, specifically a container of its legendary hummus.

When you walk into Sahadi's, you pass barrel after barrel of

olives, dried fruits, and nuts, and imported cheeses, juices, sauces, and spices from the world over. If you walk to the back, there are two counters set at right angles to each other, from which are dispensed prepared salads, pastries, sandwiches, and the greatest, smoothest, most decadent hummus this side of Mesopotamia. Sahadi's has a spicy version, which is not to be trifled with, and regular. I bought a pound of the standard hummus, silky, almost puddinglike in its creaminess, and distinctly unlike the thicker, grainy, mortarlike hummus that is so ubiquitous. It is truly one of the finest foods available in the borough.

I stopped at my friend's home, in a great building a few blocks from the westernmost end of Atlantic, and we grabbed some cold beers and headed to the roof deck. From that lofty vantage point we watched a multicolored, multiscented, multi-aged mass of people that stretched as far as the eye could see eastward to Fourth Avenue, everyone rejoicing, reveling, performing, eating and drinking, flirting and browsing, growing, and growing old. A river of beautiful Brooklyn humanity, flowing toward the river and ebbing toward Prospect Park. A Benetton-worthy cross section of the many races and peoples who give Brooklyn its undiluted power, passion, and perspective.

The crowds broke off toward their respective neighborhoods as the sun sank behind the glittery geometry of the New York skyline. Manhattan—separated by only a river from the mighty working class that pumps the blood through its veins, the beats through its speakers, and history through its very core. Just a strip of murky mystery away from the sprawling, special, and indomitable spirit of the very people who make it and the nation great. The huddled masses have taken refuge in the shadow of the Brooklyn Bridge, and in the process have formed a cultural and culinary tapestry as thrilling and tasty as any to be found in our great nation. Brooklyn, from Biggie to Dem Bums, from Greenpoint to Fort Greene, is Antic, sleepless, and hungry for more.

No Sleep Till . . .

CHICKEN SOUP

Rather than just give you a recipe from a random spot in my hometown, I'm gonna share a piece of my heart and, to be honest, a piece of any good Jewish boy's heart: Mom's chicken soup, in her own words. Without further ado, my mom, Sharon Richman:

I pick out a nice-looking chicken, usually cut in quarters and usually kosher and free range (when possible). I don't know if it's true, but psychologically I think if it had a better life, if it's killed quickly, according to tradition, and handled efficiently, the soup will taste better. (Maybe it's karma.)

I clean it under cold water and pick out any small feathers that might remain. (Adam was always very fussy about finding feathers on any chicken I served him.) Usually, I boil it for a few minutes in a small amount of water and then spill that water out.

I set the chicken aside and prepare my vegetables. I follow the advice of the many fine cooks who came before me and start with a "big onion"—usually more than one. I peel them and cut them in half or quarters, depending upon the size. I then clean the carrots (I used to "scrape" them, also known as peeling, but stopped doing that and traded in the knife for a scrub brush to preserve more nutrients). Use as many carrots as you'd like, enough to satisfy the needs of your family. Years ago, I never used leeks (whoever heard of them?) or celery root. Now I sometimes add these as well as a parsley root. I usually use turnips and parsnips and always a big bunch of washed parsley and a big bunch of dill. I don't usually make a "bouquet garni," but just wash and trim the parsley and dill and trim the roots off (of course this requires you to strain the soup before serving, so you can have a nice light golden liquid). I peel the turnips and celery root.

I always use a large, 8- to 10-quart pot for my soup, because the vegetables and chicken take up lots of space. I then add water to cover everything and, of course, coarse kosher salt to taste. After the vegetables, chicken, and water are in the pot, I cover the pot and bring the contents to a boil. I then lower the flame and simmer the soup for about 1½ hours on a medium-low flame. An Italian friend of mine has suggested putting a whole tomato in, but it's risky because you have to remove it before it bursts and sends its seeds exploding into your soup! Some other Jewish cooks I know add a powder known as "soup base" or bouillon cubes to the soup, because they say it makes it richer. (I confess, I too have done this upon RARE occasion, particularly if I thought my soup tasted too watery or not chickeny enough. But usually I won't do this. If you do, be careful which bouillon cubes you use, as some contain stuff you don't want in your soup.)

One can make matzoh balls to accompany the soup (just follow the recipe on the matzoh meal box!), but be sure to cook them SEPA-RATELY, in a covered pot of boiling water, and then add them to the soup right before serving. My matzoh balls are generally light and fluffy (supposedly highly desired and sought after), but truthfully, I and my sister and brother-in-law prefer the heavier, more solid ones. If you like them that way too, then just break all the rules and don't—whatever you do—use seltzer or club soda (reported to help keep them light) in lieu of water. Noodles, rice, broken crackers, or matzoh are good to add to the soup when serving. (Pick one or add them all, as my friend's husband does.) Most important, eat it in good health. Enjoy!!

CHAPTER 4

MEET ME FOR SUSHI IN ST. LOUIS, LOUIE: CAN IT BE JUST FAIR?

Meat, Marinara, and Mouthfuls on the Mississippi

★ ★ ★

ST. LOUIS, MO

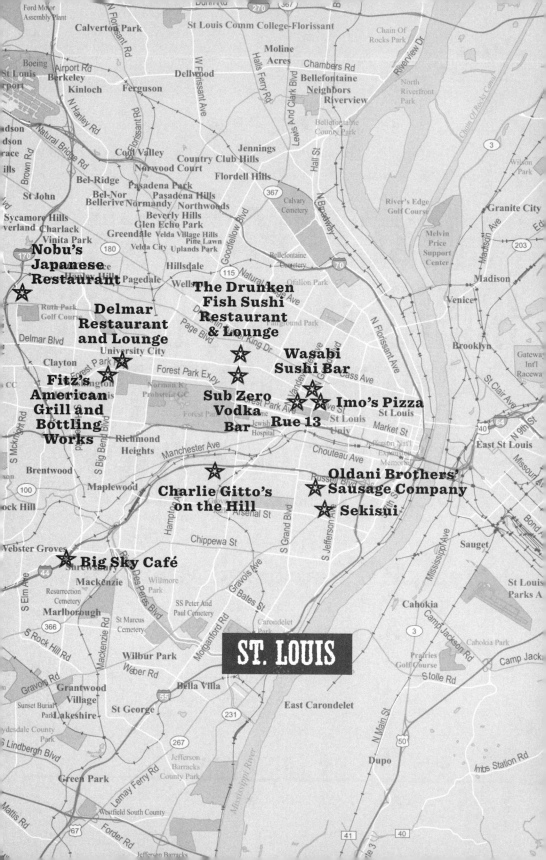

I'm at the top of the Gateway Arch and it's swaying back and forth—way more than I'm comfortable with—and I'm looking down at the Mississippi, which I wish weren't so muddy. As I cross over to the other side of the world's biggest croquet wicket, I stare out at the city through a narrow rectangular window.

One baseball stadium is being torn down, another is being built, and, at least in the Lou, the Cardinals' Albert Pujols is a god who walks the earth and allows mortals the chance to strike him out. He sits at the right hand of baseball great Ozzie Smith and in the court of legendary football player Dan Dierdorf, while the rap composer known as Nelly sings about the nearby Frontenac neighborhood as he explains that it "must be the money." That's St. Looey right thurrr.

I thought I could see everything from the top of the arch, but the more time I spent in St. Louis, the more I realized that there is more to this city than first meets the eye. The stage was set for me to learn this when an acting gig led to my relocating to the Lou in 2005.

ACT ONE
(Wherein Adam the waiter gets a job acting in St. Louis and finds a great restaurant next door to his scary apartment)

When you're an actor and the call comes saying you got the gig, your heart swells, your shoulders lighten, and you rejoice in knowing that your survival jobs can kiss your entire ass. In terms of regional theater, a job means six to eight weeks of work, regular paychecks, and baby steps toward medical insurance. Plus, when you tell someone you're an actor, you have an answer to fire back when they invariably ask, "What are you acting in *now*?" It was just such a call that first brought me to the Gateway to the West.

The gig was a three-man play called *All the Great Books* at a really good theater, with a strong role for me and two very solid cast mates. And so my days of waiting tables in New York were over—again.

Because the large cast of the previous production was still in residence at the official actor housing, when we first arrived my cast mates and I had the good fortune to be housed in the vintage splendor of the Chase Park Plaza on Kingshighway Boulevard in Central West End.

This glorious, sprawling hotel and apartment complex housed multiple restaurants and bars, as well as a movie theater and an Aveda salon. The residences were lavishly appointed, and my room had a view of the arch. My trip to the Gateway City was starting brilliantly. I lived in a hip, stylish, and thriving neighborhood where there were sushi restaurants, boutiques, vodka bars, small independent groceries, and places that sold organic free trade coffee with Death Cab for Cutie records playing in the background. It was beautiful. I could really see myself getting used to the neighborhood.

But we didn't stay long.

You see, the theater, in a very canny move, had bought an old apartment complex in Webster Groves, an inner-ring suburb close to the theater. It was directly across from train tracks and near little else, and that's where we were moved as soon as the previous cast vacated. This apartment building was old and far from the prettiest, but it was home and I lived there rent-free. Other actors had apparently named this residence the Bates Motel and Meth Lab Apartments, and for good reason. While there wasn't a murderous innkeeper or drugs being cooked up, it was a very dark, hard-to-find locale and miles away from the opulence of my first accommodations.

Whereas I had been excited to explore Central West End, I had no such desire with regard to our new neighborhood. Instead I decided to spend my time working and cooking at home, saving as much of my salary as I could.

It took a visit from my mom for me to realize how shortsighted I'd been. She had come to town to see the show and celebrate her birthday. She asked my two cast mates and me which were our favorite restaurants near the theater, and we sheepishly admitted that we either ordered in or cooked for ourselves in our little Meth Lab Apartments.

"I saw someplace lovely," she said, in her endearing Brooklynese, "right near your house, Ad."

"Where?"

"Right next door."

"Ma, that's a senior citizens' home."

"Not there, one more door down."

"What's one more door down? Where is there a door? There's that home, then a knitting store, then our rehearsal space and a Starbucks. That's it."

"No."

"What do you mean, no?"

"I mean, no, there is a place," she insisted.

"Okay, birthday girl, you lead on."

And so she did, to an inconspicuous place that was nearly obscured by trees and lack of light. A beautiful little gem known as the Big Sky Café.

We walked in and sat in the large-windowed dining room that was also part wine bar. The menu had straight-ahead solid American fare they called "Revitalized American Comfort Food," with an emphasis on seasonal ingredients and classic flavors. The wine list was terrific. I ordered the beet salad, which was roasted golden and red beets with mixed greens, local dairy Heartland Creamery's goat cheese, toasted hazelnuts, and an apricot vinaigrette.

The goat cheese was creamy with a mild herbaceous, "farmy" flavor. The smoky, buttery crunch of the hazelnuts and the bitterness of the greens were refreshing counterpoints to the sweet, chewy, almost succulent beets and fruity vinaigrette.

And I was eating this highly refreshing, skillfully made salad in the shadow of massive trees and a locomotive in the middle of a barely named street in St. Louis! Meanwhile, my cast mate was ooohing and aaahing over his rich, velvety mac and cheese—again made with milk and cheese from a local dairy. It was so thick and rich the fork could nearly stand up straight in it.

We ordered some garlic mashed potatoes for the table, which were whipped and flavorful, like a starchy vampire-repellent cloud.

And my salmon main course? Holy shit.

It had a grid of sear marks like a great steak and a beautiful soy glaze with a strong scent of ginger and was accompanied by perfectly cooked broccolini and a winter squash risotto that was every bit as hearty and comfort-food-tastic as my friend's mac and cheese.

We were eating wonderful food, drinking amazing wine (apparently, the place has won like four *Wine Spectator* awards for its cellar), in a place near a seniors' home, a thunderous cargo train track, and a yarn and craft store. A place totally obscured by trees and my own inability to see the world around me.

Big Sky Café remains one of the best comfort-food places I have ever been to—and not just because it was a mind-blowingly delicious reprieve from tuna sandwiches and ramen noodles. It served as a real wake-up call for me; there are great places to eat in the most unlikely spots—not just in our less than desirable neighborhood, but all throughout St. Louis. It is indeed a city of many parts.

★★★

Ask people what they think of when they think of St. Louis, Missouri, and they will tell of thick barbecue sauce, blues music, great baseball, the arch, maybe the Fallujah-like wilds of East St. Louis across the river in Illinois, or the several local sights that are mentioned in Tennessee Williams's works of drama. Maybe you'll get an earful about Nelly, the river, Charles Lindbergh's Spirit of St. Louis plane, or riverboat gambling.

For all those reasons and more, St. Louis is a city that occupies a prominent spot in the mythology of America. It is a city that survived both the American Revolution and the Civil War virtually untouched and became a bastion of middle-American commerce. It belonged to France, then Spain, then France again until that country sold the city along with more than 800,000 additional square miles of land (about 23% of our country today) to the United States in an acquisition known as the Louisiana Purchase. It hosted the World's Fair and Olympic Games in the same year (1904, FYI). It remains one of the greatest sports cities in the United States, a music and arts titan in the region, and the Gateway to the West.

> The river-edge area of St. Louis, like many areas along the Mississippi, is karstic, meaning that it has limestone bedrock that has dissolved in places, resulting in a wealth of springs, sinkholes, and caves. During Prohibition, these caves were used by the mob in secretly ferrying liquor up and down the river!

And as its population grows, the city's culinary profile is evolving too, largely through the integration of the various immigrant communities as well as the cuisines they brought with them.

St. Louis sits just south of the point where the Mississippi and Missouri rivers meet. The flows of both of these rivers have resulted in wide valleys with large floodplains of incredibly fertile soil. Though most of the area is prairie and valley, the city itself is built on bluffs that overlook the western bank of the muddy Mississippi.

St. Louis is at the northern edge of America's humid subtropical climate zone, so it has hot, humid summers and cool winters. But it is also right on the line of the humid continental climate zone, which is known for wildly different weather from season to season: Fall can be abnormally warm, resulting in an Indian summer; spring is very wet and prone to extreme weather, like tornadoes; summer is warm with frequent thunderstorms; and winter can be rindonkulously frigid, with frequent snowfall and temperatures regularly below freezing. (Having lived there through the holidays, I can tell you that it's so cold your balls will clink. Assuming you have them.)

Despite the somewhat erratic weather, though, St. Louis's value as a shipping hub made the city a very desirable place to live in the early 19th century. Originally, there was mining within the city limits and even some agriculture, but starting in 1817, the reliance upon steamboat shipping on the Mississippi and St. Louis's place as the northernmost navigable port for vessels of this size (dangerous rapids lay to the north) made the bustling city one of the nation's most prosperous.

Immigrants from Germany inundated St. Louis during this period, and in fact roughly 15% of the population today claims German heritage. Irish immigrants fleeing the potato famine also came in droves, and often found work in the shipping industry (and started some of the most notorious gangs of the day). And African

German immigrants shaped the local cuisine with their use of pork, and in particular bratwurst, and St. Louis's other main culinary contribution: beer. Their desserts—stollens, strudels, cakes, and pies—are not only still hugely popular, but also have modern analogues in dishes like the St. Louis specialty gooey butter cake, a type of German-style coffee cake with a soft, almost puddinglike center. (Urban legend holds that the cake was made by accident in the 1930s by a German American baker who, in a moment of innocent confusion, reversed the proportions of sugar and flour in her cake batter. Having had homemade gooey butter cookies, I can say firsthand that this is one of the best accidents ever!)

Americans from the South flooded into St. Louis as well, seeking better opportunities in what's known as the Great Migration between 1916 and 1930.

As a result of this massive influx, the population of St. Louis grew from less than 20,000 in 1840 to more than 820,000 by 1930, with the related cultural and economic gains. Later in the 19th century, Italian immigrants began to arrive to take advantage of the employment opportunities connected to nearby clay deposits.

> Baseball greats Yogi Berra and Joe Garagiola Sr. grew up in the Hill, as did five members of the amazing 1950 US soccer team that defeated England in the FIFA World Cup. (Something in the sauce perhaps?)

These immigrant communities settled in concentrated and sharply demarcated pockets that are still reflected in the city today: South St. Louis is traditionally white; the north is traditionally black. Italians are largely found in the famous Hill neighborhood; the Irish settled in the Kerry Patch section. And now, with an estimated 70,000 Bosnian immigrants having settled in and around the Bevo neighborhood in southern St. Louis, the Gateway to the West is one of the largest Bosnian diaspora communities in the country. The city also boasts a significant Polish population, and in recent years, the Thai and Vietnamese populations have been growing as well.

And all of these cultures brought their foods with them.

The Italian community, largely from Sicily and Milan, brought

Pannetone is a yeasted sweet bread studded with candied orange, lemon zest, and raisins. These dome-shaped cakes are properly allowed to rise for days, causing the dough to proof to heights of ridiculous fluffiness. Those that come in brightly colored octagonal boxes are not as good.

their very specific cooking traditions to St. Louis and filtered them through the produce and ingredients that were available to them. As a reminder: Sicilian food can be roughly categorized as what we would all consider Italian food with significant Arabic influences (couscous, citrus fruits and apricots, rice, saffron, raisins, nutmeg, and cinnamon, for example), yielding dishes like rice balls and caponata (deeply flavored eggplant salad). Milanese cuisine is unique among the Italian cuisines in that it uses virtually no tomatoes and prefers rice to pasta. It has given us dishes like osso buco and cassoeula (the latter being stewed pork rib chops and sausage with cabbage, not unlike the German stews made all over St. Louis) and baked goods like the Christmas cake pannetone.

Using these influences, the Italian community in St. Louis created two significant dishes: toasted ravioli and St. Louis–style pizza.

Toasted ravioli, sometimes known locally as t-ravs, consist of meat or cheese wrapped in a pasta square that is breaded and deep-fried until it becomes crispy and golden brown. Toasted ravioli can be found all over menus in the Hill. In fact, two different

Ten More Great Places for Pizza Outside New York

1. Sally's, Frank Pepe's, & Modern Apizza—New Haven, CT (They're all great—some places do certain pies better than others)
2. Lou Malnati's—Chicago, IL
3. Pizzeria Bianco—Phoenix, AZ
4. Flying Pie—Boise, ID
5. Maruca's—Seaside Heights, NJ
6. Galleria Umberto—Boston, MA
7. Tacconelli's—Philadelphia, PA
8. 2 Amys—Washington, DC
9. Pizzeria Mozza—Los Angeles, CA
10. Pizzeria Delfina—San Francisco, CA

restaurants in the Hill still continue to claim that their chefs originated t-ravs in the early 1940s: Terry Hill at Oldani's restaurant and Charlie Gitto at the restaurant that bears his name. The truth is still unknown.

St. Louis–style pizza is known primarily for three things: its super-thin yeastless crust, a topping of Provel cheese (Provel is a brand name for a blend of provolone, Swiss, and white Cheddar) instead of mozzarella, and servings cut into little, square pieces rather than wedges. There also tends to be a touch more oregano in St. Louis pies than elsewhere. The incredibly sweet (and tasty) sauce is said to be a direct product of the Sicilian influence on the Italian foods of St. Louis.

As a thin-crust devotee, I have to say that St. Louis pizza is delicious; in fact, the pies dished up by local chain Imo's taste like angel tears dipped in happiness—and make any bottle of wine spectacular.

While any self-respecting rundown of St. Louis's culinary contributions would have to include the St. Paul sandwich—an egg foo yong sandwich available in the city's Chinese restaurants—and the delicious slinger—a morning-after and post-party dish of eggs, bacon, breakfast chili, cheese, and onion reminiscent of Rochester, New York's "garbage plate"—you cannot talk about St. Louis food without touching on St. Louis–style barbecue.

St. Louis is regarded by many as a barbecue mecca. It bears noting that the local flora includes a pit master's greatest hits in terms of smoking woods: oak, maple, and hickory. Add to this the fact that all of the cultures that converged on St. Louis came with their own meat-cooking traditions, and the stage was clearly set to create a lasting charred-meat legacy.

St. Louis–style barbecue is a broad term that encompasses all the varied styles in the Lou's neighborhoods. While the city is known for crazy barbecue delicacies like crispy snoots (charred pig snouts and cheeks), the most popular are pork ribs (more often than not spareribs) and pork steaks (sliced rounds of pork butt or shoulder that are cut and served like steaks).

What really defines 'cue in the Lou, though, is its sauce and the liberal application thereof. Ribs are cooked for a long time at low temperatures and basted with sauce throughout, creating a caramelized shell and a deep, penetrating flavor. Pork steaks, on the other hand, tend to be grilled over extremely high heat and then slow-simmered in sauce and beer to tenderize and flavor the meat, or seared and then slow-smoked, the way ribs are, before being doused in the sauce.

So let's talk about the sauce.

St. Louis–style barbecue sauce is almost always tomato based, sometimes incorporating mustard and molasses, with some vinegar to thin it out and play off the sweetness of the tomato and molasses. Often the flavor is punched up with cayenne, garlic, and even dehydrated onion. It's easy to confuse this sauce with that preferred by pitmasters in nearby Kansas City, but KC sauce is way thicker and sweeter than St. Louis's is, and the sauce favored by fellow barbecue titan Texas is generally way hotter and almost water thin. In neither of those places is the meat slathered with sauce as lavishly as in St. Looey.

And that's the thing, nobody does what St. Louis does quite like it does it: not barbecue, not blues, not baseball. It is a city that is growing by leaps and bounds in terms of population, cultural significance, and cultural richness. It boasts an amazing symphony, great theaters, and a history rich enough to sink your teeth into.

It is the Gateway to the West, the city that offered inspiration equally to Josephine Baker and Lewis and Clark. The city where rivers and generations of Americans have met and flourished and flowed into a great tradition on the western bank of the Mississippi, one that is generously coated with hearty layers of tradition, heart, and sticky-sweet, wonderful, wonderful sauce.

All of which is to say that while there is wonderful eating to be done in St. Louis, you'd never suffer any illusion that you were in, say, New York or LA or even Chicago when you were doing it, for better or worse. As I found out the hard way when I got the hare-brained notion of trying to find sushi in the Gateway city.

ACT TWO
(Wherein a trip to the Delmar Loop leads to great music and an amazing burger and root beer)

After my show at the regional theater had been running a few weeks. I needed to break out of Webster Groves, where we'd been rehearsing and performing. As I'd been given a company car, I headed down to the Delmar Loop, not too far from Washington University in St. Louis's University City neighborhood—a school I nearly attended and whose students can be found on Delmar carousing at places like Blueberry Hill, the Pageant (where I saw Nelly perform), and the Pin-Up Bowl.

I parked at a lot at Big Bend and Delmar and decided to go for a walk, stopping in several boutiques and specialty shops geared toward the youth of the Lou—and toward siphoning a part of Mommy and Daddy's money from the Wash U student body. There are myriad restaurants on the Loop: Latin places selling subpar mofongo; great Ethiopian spots that play world music into the wee hours of the night; yogurt spots; a place with a customizable Bloody Mary bar that does a great jazz brunch; and Imo's, which serves an amazing thin-crust, almost creamy cheese-laden St. Louis–style pizza. I was overwhelmed. I happened to look in the window of a place called the Delmar Lounge. It seemed like a chill spot, with booths, a bar, and dark red, brown, and black décor.

"Hey, you're the actor dude!"

I turned to see an Asian guy in his late 20s setting up his turntables in the corner. He looked familiar, but I couldn't place his face at first. "Hersh, bro," he said, introducing himself. "I met you at Euclid Records in Webster Groves. I work there. I sold you the

Death from Above album. And the Chiks record a few days ago." (Dear reader: "Chiks," often written as "Chk Chk Chk," is the common pronunciation for the band that calls itself !!!)

He told me a bit about the gig he was setting up for and said he'd start spinning in a few hours, but my mind was on where I should go to eat.

"What are you in the mood for?" he asked. "Oh wait, you're a sushi chef, right?" He remembered my telling him what I did before arriving in town, and apparently sushi chef made more of an impression than waiting tables.

"Yeah, but not sushi tonight. What's dope and local?"

"You been to Fitz's?"

"Whassat?" I asked.

"It's like a St. Louis legend. Where you parked?"

"Big Bend and Delmar."

"Dude, you walked right by it." You've got to be kidding me! Again? "It's a big brick building with 'Fitz's' on the side. It's a soda and root beer factory—and their burgers and onion rings are insane."

I left and walked back toward my car, toward yet another amazing restaurant I'd apparently overlooked. And sure enough, right there a block from my car, at Leland and Delmar, was a massive brick structure with the word *Fitz's* emblazoned on the side.

I learned later there was a reason I had thought Fitz's American Grill and Bottling Works was a bank. In the '30s and '40s that building had housed the Delmar Bank. The building was built in 1928 and remodeled in 1944, when an art deco façade was added, and that design remains intact today. But the outside is only half the story at Fitz's. When you walk in, the first thing you notice is the massive bottling line that spans a good third of the entire building. Long conveyors stretch for yards, sending single-file lines of root beer and cream soda bottles to be filled and packed. It's amazing to see how much industry goes into something as homey as root beer.

As I was there alone, I took a seat at the bar. I am an avowed root beer junkie, so there was no way I was missing St. Louis's root beer crown jewel. I ordered a classic bacon cheeseburger and some onion rings. The root beer came out *on draft*. It was creamy and sweet, but not overly so, and completely worth the trip.

The burger was nearly an inch thick, totally juicy, and got a *huge* boost of flavor from a Fitz's burger addition known as fried onion tanglers—thin fried onion straws that straddle the flavor line between sautéed onions and onion rings.

And speaking of onion rings, those too were incredible, about as thick and fat around as a bracelet. Seriously. The coating was fried to crispy perfection and not at all greasy. Each one was about the size of a doughnut and just as delicious.

I had a cream soda afterward, just to have a basis of comparison for the root beer. I ultimately decided that, while the cream soda was good, Fitz's is root beer country. I didn't have time for a tour of the facilities, but I promised myself that I would definitely do so in the future. I paid and waddled my happy beef, bacon, onion, and sarsaparilla ass back down Delmar to the corner of Eastgate and the Delmar Lounge.

There was Hersh, crushing it on the ones and twos, mixing in a rare Playboys record with Eric B. and Rakim. In one corner, famed producer Jazze Pha, swathed in fur and honeys, was holding court. I grabbed a drink, placed one hamburger-heavy hip against the bar, and bobbed my head to the beat. Delicious, delicious Delmar. You have fed me and you have funked me. But damn, delicious Delmar, it was time for me to eat a little lighter. As I leaned against that bar, I swore, as God's my witness, I will never eat heavy again.

From now on, "my thoughts be sushi, or be nothing worth!" as Hamlet declared, sort of. Surely it must be possible to find good sushi in the middle of our country.

ACT THREE

(Wherein Adam seeks out sushi in St. Louis, with some less than positive results)

Once the show was up and running, we did six performances a week, with Mondays off. As a cast of just three, we each had our own dresser and 30 to 40 costume changes apiece. We ran and ran and ran. We were tired.

This did not, however, at all deter us from going out.

Two of us found ourselves at the cavernous bar on Washington Avenue called Rue 13. The place was packed and looked like a hipster grenade had exploded. I recognized a few salespeople from the trendy boutiques on Delmar, and I saw Hersh and a few other guys who worked at that amazing record shop in Webster Groves, Euclid Records. There were cute girls and scruffy, unpolished dudes everywhere.

"Hey, Hersh, it always this crowded?" I asked.

"Just the Wednesday night jump-off, my man."

"Y'all just need to get out like this hard-core on a Wednesday?"

"St. Louis, man. We drink here."

"I see. What do I get?"

"They have dollar sake shots."

Slow the fuck down. I love sake. Love it. I try to learn as much as I can about it as often as I can. And though I'm no expert, I do know this: One-dollar sake *cannot be good sake*. I don't care what you say. If it were good, they wouldn't give it away for a dollar, would they? They wouldn't serve it from—no shit—squirt sport bottles, would they?

And then I glanced around at the roomful of very tall, strong-looking, beautiful women and dudes in flannel, corduroys, and knit watch caps with moustaches both legitimate and ironic and I thought, "Stop being a snob. Do a shot."

I coerced my cast mate into doing a shot or two with me and we chose from the seemingly endless list of flavors, all of which would be blasphemous to any self-respecting sake lover, including melons, berries, what have you.

Plastic shot glasses down. Squirt bottles up. *Squuuuuuuush!*

Bright pink liquid shot into two medicine dose cups. Somewhere a sake distiller contemplated seppuku.

We knocked them back. The only way I can describe the flavor is something like sake punch.

"Whoa," my friend said.

"I know, dude."

"Like, intensely sweet."

"Beyond. Just beyond."

[A pause.]

"Wanna do another?"

This visit to Rue 13 happened a few years ago. I've been back since, and not only is the sushi rockin now under a new chef, but the burlesque show also has found its legs. A must-hit in St. Louis!

"Like, four."

Eight plastic cups, eight rainbow-colored shots later, and we, too, were midflight in the Wednesday night jump-off. "Dude, I'm hungry," I said.

"You sure you wanna eat this late, Adam? I mean, you wear those short shorts in the play." I did. And they sucked.

I looked over his right shoulder and gasped with joy at what I saw there: an Asian man behind a small countertop of wood and glass. And only one kind of food is served at a counter like that.

ME AS "THE COACH"

"How 'bout, sushi? That's not a bad thing to eat late, is it?"

"I don't know . . . um, how good could it be at a place with dollar sake?"

"Screw it. I'm taking my chances." And I did. I went basic: three pieces of salmon sushi, two pieces of tuna sushi, one piece of yellowtail. We waited, talking the utter shit that two actors talk when they're drunk—auditions, directors, basically singing the rhapsodies of the catty, clever, opinionated, and vain—and having a ball.

And then my sushi came.

It looked innocent enough. Simple, clean, straight-down-the-middle sushi.

I bit into the salmon. No smell, but no taste either, just somewhat fatty and not altogether cold enough.

I bit into the tuna. Nice iron-y flavor, but a bit fibrous and stringy.

I tried to take a bite of the yellowtail, but it resisted.

"How's the sushi?"

"Not happening. More sake?"

"More sake!"

We ended up meeting some folks and staying for the burlesque show in the back.

Now, I can acknowledge the cattiness of actors watching other performers, but this show was just not working. One girl wiped out big-time doing some contortionist shtick, and the "fire-breather" did not aspirate and spray the fluid at the flame to create a fireball centerpiece, but rather spat a stream and extinguished it.

"This is burl-*esque*."

"It's burl-*ish*."

We were being catty and we knew it. We needed to leave.

That weekend, we decided to head back to the hip, stylish, and more expensive Central West End, where I had seen several sushi places during my brief stay there.

We started at a place on Euclid, not far from our old digs at the exquisite Chase Park Plaza. A vodka bar lit like a scene from *Blade Runner*, with a bar that literally was covered in frost, like inside a freezer. A place full of biceps and low-waisted jeans displaying a hint of thong and tramp stamp, and a staggeringly impressive vodka selection. It was called Sub Zero.

We amused ourselves at the frosty bar, leaving handprints on it and whatnot, and knocked back some incredible, crystalline clear potables from the world over. Already, our drink experience was clicking along, so when I saw the sushi counter in the corner of the bar, I smiled broadly.

At last. I was gonna get my rawness on.

As before, I went ultrasimple. One tuna roll, two pieces of salmon sushi.

I should mention again how hot the clientele was, how great

the vodka selection was, and how well informed and cool the staff were.

I want to do this to soften the blow of my next statement.

The sushi fucking sucked.

Texture, taste, color—all off.

I excused myself from the establishment, needing to take the air.

I inhaled the crisp, wintry Missouri air.

I exhaled one piece of tuna roll and two pieces of salmon sushi. Epic. Sushi. Fail.

I walked back up Euclid, sheepishly mopping the corners of my mouth with my handkerchief.

As I rejoined my friends, I looked at a darkly lit place directly across the street from Sub Zero that was pumping some solid drum and bass and had a sign that read: Drunken Fish.

"Guess they make sushi," said my friend.

"Please don't talk about sushi," I responded feebly.

For the next week and a half it was oatmeal and dry turkey sandwiches for me. No lie.

But the itch to go out would not be denied, and I had met a cute lawyer who seemed just as determined as I was to find good sushi. So, again I went to Central West End, this time to the aforementioned Drunken Fish, which unlike my earlier destinations was a restaurant first and a nightlife institution second. That had to count for something, right?

We walked in and posted up at the sushi bar.

Not one of the sushi chefs was Asian.

Gulp.

But then again, being a sushi maker myself and about as Asian as David Carradine, maybe I was being hypocritical.

We opened the drink menu. I wanted sake. Having worked in many sushi restaurants, I was eagerly anticipating a variety of sake—either different brands or different levels of purity (junmai, daiginjo, and so on).

Um, no.

They offered hot or cold, and large or small.

Gulp.

The waitress saw me looking at the menu. Perhaps she read my consternation as confusion. She pointed to the Korean soju that was inexplicably on the menu and offered this little pearl of wisdom: "Yo, that's the shit that gets you stupid!"

I challenge any sommelier to bring the thunder like that ("Ah yes, the Penfolds Grange is the shit that's so dope you wanna donkey punch your grandma. Tannins for days, dawg!").

As much as I like getting stupid, a first date isn't the right time for that, so I ordered sake, a "cold, large," and hoped for the best.

We went for two pieces of salmon and tuna sushi each.

The sake came first. I quaffed it and felt warm and optimistic.

And I'm happy to say that, while not groundbreakingly awesome, the sushi at the Drunken Fish was solid enough that we were emboldened to order some rolls, too. While certain "signature" rolls were clearly playing to the comfort-food palate of the region, incorporating lots of cream cheese, tempura, and even cheesesteak, they also used some surprising ingredients, like seared tuna, honey-wasabi mayo, and asparagus.

It turned out to be a very good meal in a fun setting.

After we ate, we went upstairs and did awful karaoke versions of Journey and Foreigner songs, then cabbed it home.

All in all a good night, but as a former Angeleno and current New Yorker who's experienced higher degrees of sushi nirvana in far lesser locales, I wondered: Is that really the best this berg has to offer, sushi wise?

Can there be more than just okay sushi to feed this quintessence of dust?

Can sushi creep in this petty pace from day to day to the last syllable of recorded time in St. Louis?

Alas, good sushi—I knew it well.

ACT FOUR

(Wherein Adam stumbles upon the best fishmonger he's ever encountered and learns that home is where the hamachi is)

Two weeks to go until the end of the run.

The reviews had been awesome. And the cast has bonded both as an ensemble and as a formidable attack squad in Star Wars Battlefront on one of the guys' Xbox.

I was now seeing my cute lawyer friend regularly (although she would eventually stop talking to me, but that's another story).

I had bought some great artwork.

Had seen the ridiculously amazing holiday light display at Tilles Park.

Had spent a day, so cold any normal person would rather have been indoors, with the entire amazing St. Louis Zoo to myself. (And it was every bit as awesome as it sounds.)

Had had my picture in the *Riverfront Times*. Twice.

But my sushi yearnings had not been quelled. One day I was killing time before meeting the lawyer for a cup of coffee and was wandering about on Brentwood, a major shopping thoroughfare not far from her home.

Along the street were massive sporting goods stores, bookstores, and so on. I bought a copy of the next play I was to do—Mark Harelik's *The Immigrant*—and as I walked on I found myself a bit peckish. Whole Foods is always good for a few free samples here and there, so I popped in and ambled amidst the aisles of amaranth and toasted walnut vinegar.

I happened into the seafood section and snacked for a bit on little samples of their amazing seafood stews, soups, and chowders. I looked guiltily over at the fishmongers, who must have seen me treating myself to a free meal, and meandered over to make small talk and perhaps make amends for my freeloading.

There, something called salmon candy caught my eye. I asked a young fishmonger what it was. He said, "Dude, I'll let you try some, but you're gonna hate me, because it's expensive and you'll be addicted." I laughed and tossed the morsel of coppery orange, flaky fish into my mouth.

In a word: orgasmic. Sweet, smoky, slightly fishy, with a richness that bordered on buttery.

> In terms of sushi in St. Louis, since my interlude there, great strides have been made. Places like Yoshi's, Wasabi, Nobus, and Sekisui have been garnering accolades for great sushi not just within St. Louis, but also on the national stage.

I thanked him for yet another free sample of aquatic deliciousness. "New York?" he asked.

"That obvious?"

"Your accent—and your Yankees hat."

"You got me."

"You liking St. Louis?"

"It's great, man. But I've been having the damnedest time finding good sushi. I guess you just can't get good fish in the middle of
the country unless it's dried like that salmon candy."

"Who says?"

"My palate and some way better experiences elsewhere. Heck,
I make my own damn sushi, and it's been better than what I've
found so far. It's got to be the fish."

"Dude, I can get you great fish," he said.

"Come on, you have to say that! You're a fishmonger for Whole
Foods and you're trying to push merchandise."

"Nah, bro. I take pride in this stuff. What you looking for,
tuna?"

"What's fresh?"

"I won't even mention it to you if it isn't the best. Bluefin good?
Yellowfin?"

"You can get sushi-grade tuna?"

"How much you need?"

"Dude, please. If someone has awesome fish like you claim to,
why aren't they serving it everywhere?"

"Cost, maybe? Dunno. But we can get great seafood in St. Louis.
Don't fool yourself."

"Sushi grade?"

"Just tell me how much."

I was skeptical, I was wary.

"Quarter pound. Whichever is freshest."

"Done. See you tomorrow."

Okay, I thought, what do I have to lose? Once more into the wasabi, dear friends. I met my cute lawyer friend for coffee and told her that tomorrow night we'd have sushi at my place, by my hand. Come hell, high water, or heaving. I told her to bring an Imo's St. Louis–style pizza as "meal insurance."

The next day, I arrived at the fish counter and did not see my fishmonger friend.

Uh-oh.

"Umm, hi. I ordered some fish yesterday?" I asked a slightly older fishmonger.

"Let me check in the back."

After a few minutes that felt like ages, I heard, "Hey Brooklyn! You're back!" It was my guy emerging from the prep kitchen.

"So? You got something for me?"

"I do," he beamed. And he produced a diamond-shaped, plastic-wrapped piece of tuna that looked *exactly* like a large ruby. No flaws, a bright yet deep red color, and firm.

Splendid and on par with any fish I had purchased on either the West or the East Coast. "I looked at what came in, and while this is usually when we get great yellowtail, the yellowfin looked better. Trust me."

I did. I also bought a green onion and an avocado, some nori and wasabi, and a bag of medium-grain Calrose rice, then went home to prepare my sushi.

Unable to resist, I sliced a thin piece off the wedge and popped it into my mouth. Clean, firm, yet succulent. Zero smell and a pleasing minerality. Possibly some of the best tuna I've come across.

I made rolls, hand rolls, and nigiri sushi and sliced up bits of sashimi. We ate heartily and laughed, trying to wrap our heads around how we got such incredible fish in St. Louis and how we would stay in touch once I went back home. (We didn't, but we did have the pizza for breakfast the next morning.)

So maybe the finest sushi I ate in the city was in my own damn kitchen, but still, it could not have happened without the resources of the Lou. This experience taught me to value the advice of local marketers more than I ever had before, but I also learned that it takes work to find the best eats in new places. Whether it be a restaurant or great ingredients, attention must be paid.

[Exeunt omnes.]

FINIS

HOMEMADE SUSHI

This recipe comes from my experience as a sushi chef in New York and in my own kitchen. I offer it less as a taste of St. Louis than as a reminder of what I learned during my time living there: that you can find great food almost anywhere. You just have to keep an open mind and sometimes put in some work to locate it. This recipe also makes for a perfect dinner to prepare if you're having someone special over—it's pretty easy, it's light, and you can even feed each other!

The keys to good sushi are great fish and well-prepared rice. Nigiri sushi, which is shaped by hand, is easier to make than rolls for novice sushi chefs, and you can make it with nearly any kind of fish you prefer. When picking out your fish, be sure to purchase it from a fishmonger you trust and ask for the freshest "sashimi-grade" fish they have. You should be able to find sashimi-grade tuna or salmon at your local market or at a Japanese specialty shop.

> 1 cup rice wine vinegar
>
> ¼ cup sugar
>
> 2 tablespoons salt
>
> 1 4-inch piece kombu seaweed or kelp (optional)
>
> 2 cups sushi rice (or any short-grain white rice) uncooked
>
> 12 ounces (or more) sashimi-grade tuna
>
> Wasabi paste
>
> Soy sauce

Making the rice is easy. In a small pot over medium-low heat, combine the vinegar, sugar, salt, and kombu (if using). Heat until the sugar and salt dissolve, then remove from the heat and discard the kombu. Let sit at room temperature or in the refrigerator for at least 2 hours.

Cook the rice according to the package directions, either in a saucepan or an electric rice cooker.

When the rice is done, place it in a glass or wooden bowl. Add the vinegar mixture and use a fork or a flat wooden spoon to cool down the rice and work in the seasonings, spreading and turning the rice with a gentle slashing motion; do not stir. Cover with a cloth towel and keep warm.

Thoroughly clean a cutting board and place the fish on it. Using a sharp knife, cut your tuna into thin slices (about 3 centimeters wide). Don't worry about doing this as well as the sushi chefs you've seen—you won't be able to! Sushi chefs train for years to get this right. Just try to slice the fish into the nicest, neatest pieces that you can. Using a small spoon or your fingers, dot each piece of tuna with a pea-size dab of wasabi paste.

Forming the rice is a little trickier than it might seem. Your rice will be very sticky, so you need to wet your hands between each piece. Using one hand as a cup, place a small portion of the rice (about the size of your thumb) in your palm, and then use two fingers of your other hand to shape it into a long oval. The bottom should be flat and the top and sides rounded. Again, you needn't shape them perfectly. Just try to make somewhat symmetrical pieces so they all look about the same. Make as many rice ovals as you have tuna slices.

Lay the fish on top gently, wasabi side down (that is what's going to help it stick), and then press it firmly onto the rice. Serve with an additional dot of wasabi and a small bowl of soy sauce.

Remember, dip your fish in the soy, not the rice, and place it in your mouth fish-side down.

✯ ✯ ✯

CHAPTER 5

I STILL CALL IT THE JAKE

Or: How I Learned to Stop Worrying and Love the Browns

✯ ✯ ✯

CLEVELAND, OH

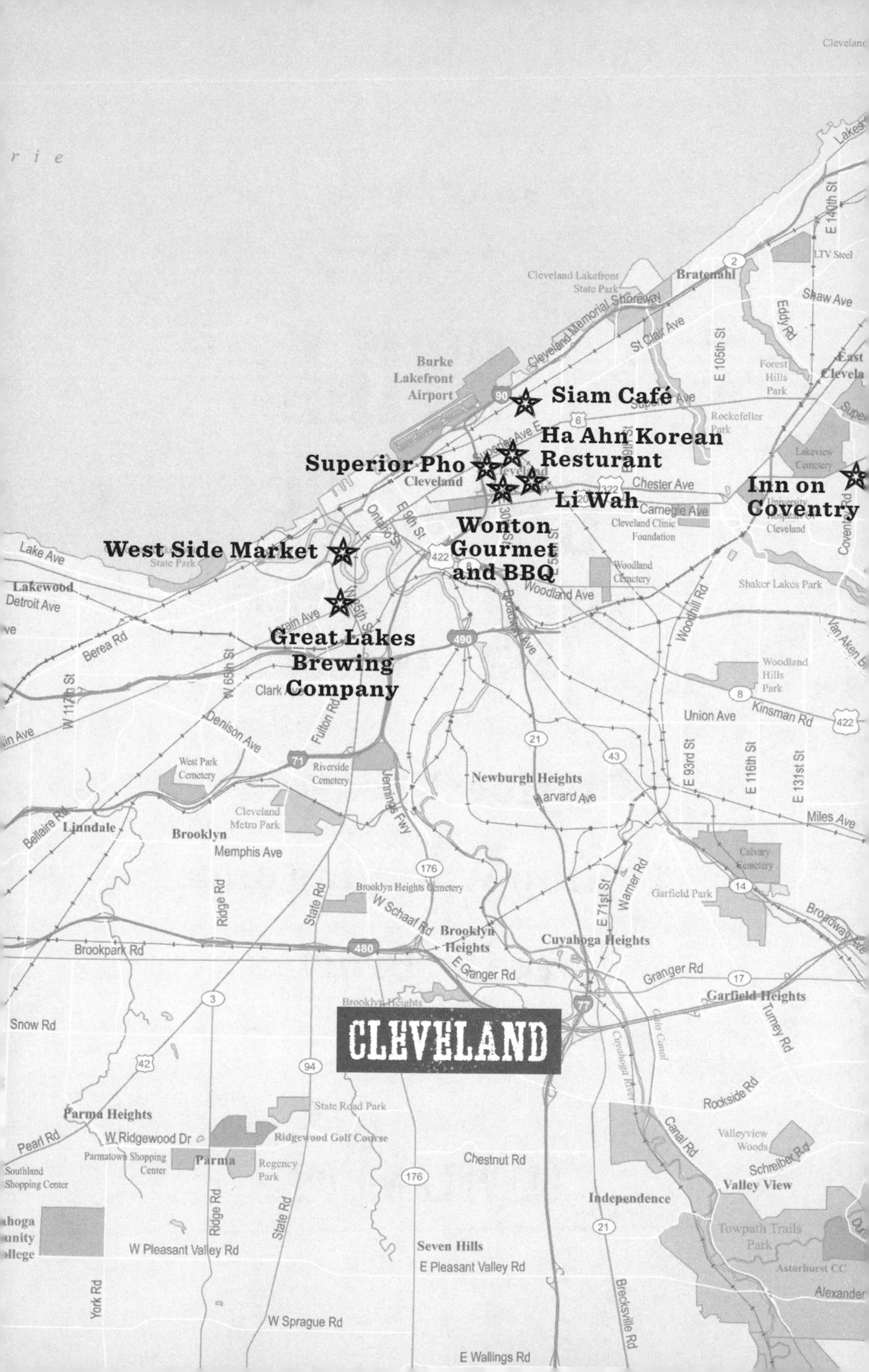

CLEVELAND
Siam Café
Ha Ahn Korean Resturant
Superior Pho
Li Wah
Inn on Coventry
Wonton Gourmet and BBQ
West Side Market
Great Lakes Brewing Company
Burke Lakefront Airport
Cleveland Lakefront State Park
Bratenahl
Lakewood
Linndale
Brooklyn
Newburgh Heights
Brooklyn Heights
Cuyahoga Heights
Garfield Heights
Parma Heights
Parma
Independence
Valley View
Seven Hills
Cleveland Clinic Foundation
Woodland Cemetery
Shaker Lakes Park
Riverside Cemetery
West Park Cemetery
Cleveland Metro Park
Calvary Cemetery
Garfield Park
Towpath Trails Park
Ridgewood Golf Course
State Road Park
Brookpark Rd
Granger Rd
Chester Ave
Carnegie Ave
Woodland Ave
Union Ave
Kinsman Rd
Miles Ave
Lorain Ave
Detroit Ave
Lake Ave
Memphis Ave
Snow Rd
W Pleasant Valley Rd
E Pleasant Valley Rd
W Sprague Rd
E Wallings Rd
Chestnut Rd
Rockside Rd

The weather: rainy, cold, and shitty. The day: Monday. The place: Cleveland. This was my first time back in two and a half years. Back then, I wasn't some visitor staying at a downtown hotel with a *Christmas Story* leg lamp in the lobby and brochures for the Great Lakes Science Center and the Rock and Roll Hall of Fame on every horizontal surface. No. Back then, I was a resident appearing in a long-running play at the Cleveland Play House, a contributing member of society who had a mailing address and a discount card at the local grocery store and was enriching the city's coffers with my taxes and fines from the traffic tickets that one could so easily acquire courtesy of the bullshit traffic light surveillance cameras on Carnegie and Euclid. I lived in Shaker Heights, worked out in Richmond, worked near the Cleveland Clinic, drank on Cedar, and flirted with the handsome, hard-drinking women on Sixth Street and Coventry. I watched games at the Jake, albeit on the jumbotron (and yes, I'll root for *anyone* who plays against Boston). I bought delicious vegetables and honey at the Shaker Heights farmers' market. I ate . . . well.

But now I was back, with two and half years between me and the soul-sucking grind of regional theater. And this time I was experiencing Cleveland with two things I lacked the last time around: money in my pocket and time to explore. Fortunately, one thing from my past remained unchanged: my friendship with a talented pianist named Erin from the Cleveland Institute of Music. We had met at a house party during my previous tenure in the Cleve and bonded over the fact that we were both Yalies and both lovers of hip-hop, in particular of A Tribe Called Quest. Erin was still in Cleveland behind the eighty-eights. As Jay-Z says, "Ladies is pimps too," and this girl has a comprehensive knowledge of the city, a rapacious appetite for good food, and the ability to make the most mundane stuff piss-in-your-pants funny. I was psyched that she would be my companion for much of my stay.

Now, this was December in Cleveland, so I'll let you guess what the weather was like, but the amount of stuff you can do here in a weekend for virtually no cash at all is awesome. I'd driven in from Pittsburgh that day, and because I firmly believe that most rest-stop food—and virtually all airport fare—should be outlawed by the Geneva Conventions, I was hungry from a day of travel. My tank was empty and so was my belly.

I picked up Erin and we headed out for some Cleve eats. Erin is of Japanese descent, and not only does she have a proclivity for Asian food, she usually knows the best spots to find it. We headed straight down St. Clair into the heart of Cleveland's AsiaTown and ended up at the Siam Café.

The room was surprisingly spacious, with pure *Miami Vice*–era mauve and neon décor. The menu was an interesting mix of Thai, Cantonese, and even some Vietnamese dishes, printed on well-worn laminated sheets with koi fish along the border. Ingredients ranged from the usual shrimp, chicken, and lobster to more left-of-center choices like live frog. Since I'm a pretty big Kermit fan, the pollywog got a stay of execution.

We ordered Tod Mun, four beautifully fried, green-onion-laden ground chicken patties with a delicious relish and ground peanuts. It was standard fare for a Thai restaurant, and though fried, it was light, not leaden, and yet substantial enough to feel like comfort food.

So far, so good. And then, Erin recommended the jellyfish. Now, you may be wondering why, when I said no to the frog, I would even contemplate chomping on a venomous invertebrate, but I was eating with a person whose opinion I trusted and whose palate I believed in, and, unlike frog (which actually does taste like chicken), I'd never tasted jellyfish before. It arrived looking like a big plate of orange fettuccine with sesame seeds. I shrugged, scooped up

a chopstickful of the orange stringiness, took a bite and . . . did not like it. It had the crunchy, cartilaginous texture of the pig ears I'd eaten in Puerto Rican restaurants back home, another dish I did not much care for.

"Erin, why did you make me order this?" I demanded.

"It's good," she insisted.

"It's not good."

"Yes it is, did you eat it with the pickles?"

"Pickles?" I asked, scanning the table for the green, dilly wonderfulness my Jewish New York upbringing had conjured in my mind. "What pickles?"

"These," she said, smiling her lovely smile and lifting a bunch of french-fry-size pieces of carrot and radish from beneath the pile of shredded jellyfish.

"Eat them together?" I asked.

"Yes, a little of each." Okay—you go, girl, I was gonna try. I forced myself to grab a bunch of the pickled veggies and a pinch of the crunchy jelly and popped it in my mouth. And it was good. Very good, in fact; actually, excellent. Without the pickles, I found the jellyfish unbearable, but with the pickles' different kind of crunch and sweet/sour flavor coupled with the hint of sesame, it was a refreshing, crisp, and very cool eating first for yours truly.

On to the main event. We'd ordered two dishes I'd never

before encountered, and bear in mind that I live in a city with no fewer than *three* Chinatowns and I was looking at a menu in *Cleveland*. The first was soup with winter melon, which I was super jazzed to try, as the notion of cold melon in hot soup was a new one to me, followed by the Spicy Salted Seafood (the waiter's recommendation).

The soup arrived in a bowl the size of the Stanley Cup. It had strands of egg like your typical egg drop soup, gumball-size pieces of bright green melon, and a mix of plump seafood and pork chunks. Absolutely splendid. The sweetness of the melon, which was surprisingly firm despite being in a cauldron of soup, was a pleasant contrast to the creaminess of the broth.

And the Spicy Salted Seafood? Fucking ridiculous, my friend. Large scallops, what I think may have been conch, head-on prawns, and who knows what else with chopped bits of fresh green onion in a dish that was not at all greasy, not even salty somehow, and had only a hint of spice. The spice worked against the richness of the seafood; the crunch of the salt crust worked against the moistness within. The dish was a revelation. Amazing and a definite must-order when I return (and, like MacArthur, I shall).

Erin had a recital to perform, so I went for a drive along the lake. Soon after passing the magnificent Rock and Roll Hall of Fame, I passed the stadium that is home to the Browns. There was clearly a game going on—you can see right into the stadium from the road—but loads of people were walking away from the venue, and I wondered if it was nearly over. I asked a man bundled in orange and brown if it was worth trying to snag a seat. I'm a huge football fan and had never seen a game in the Cleve, so it would have been worth it to grab a ticket if only for one quarter. He replied, "It ain't over, but it may as well be. Damn Browns. Chargers are killin' em. Damn Browns." And off he

CLEVELAND BROWNS FANS: THE SADDEST PEOPLE IN THE WORLD

walked. I decided to give it a go anyway, so I parked the car and hoofed it over to the stadium, fighting my way through oceans of sad, cold members of the Cleveland Browns' Dawg Pound walking in the opposite direction. The ticket taker saw me entering in the fourth quarter with the home team losing and asked, "Are you sure?" I had to laugh.

I grabbed a seat and watched Brady Quinn march the Browns down the field to a TD. The small crowd that remained cheered, but sadly, it was too little too late. I left the stadium feeling the weight of the loss like a pregnant woman's husband feels sympathy pains. But true to the plucky spirit of C-town, all you could hear was "It's all right. We'll get the Steelers next week. Only bitches wave around little yellow towels!" You can't keep a good city down, I guess.

I headed back to my hotel and watched *A Christmas Story* on TV, a movie that famously takes place in Cleveland and is the unofficial state movie (more on that later). This viewing was not serendipitous, by the way; the hotel has the film on constant repeat 24/7 during Christmas season—and yes, I watched it multiple times. I went to bed dreaming of salted seafood and getting off spectacular hip shots with my Red Ryder carbine-action 200-shot range model air rifle.

Five Great Food Films

1. Big Night (1996)
2. Moonstruck (1987)
3. Goodfellas (1990)
4. Like Water for Chocolate (1992)
5. Willy Wonka and the Chocolate Factory (1971)

★ ★ ★

As someone who once lived and worked in Cleveland, I have a particular fondness for this city. We all love a comeback—think of Rocky, Robert Downey Jr., the Karate Kid fighting and triumphing with his hobbled "swept" leg—and Cleveland truly epitomizes the comeback. The world-weary slugger, once battered, bruised, and left for dead, has risen like a phoenix on the shores of Lake Erie, shaking off the dust of urban blight, white flight, financial ruin, a flaming river, and some of the most dogged and downtrodden sports franchises in history. Today, it's home to a thriving arts community, several Beaux Arts skyscrapers, arguably one of the finest orchestras in the land, plus an arts complex that rivals Lincoln Center and a culinary profile that rivals, and at times bests, those of nearby midwestern metropolises like Chicago.

So let's address the dark phase of Cleveland's history. After all, with a nickname like the Mistake on the Lake, it's kind of the elephant in the room, and to appreciate where the Cleve is today, you need to understand just where it's come from.

Cleveland was named for General Moses Cleaveland, who led a team of surveyors from the Connecticut Land Company in laying out the downtown area. Today's Public Square was modeled after early New England towns and was initially designated as a common pasture for settlers' animals. After Cleaveland's work was done, he left, never to return to Ohio again—Cleveland's first incident of white flight.

Cleveland is surrounded by many bodies of water, notably Lake Erie, the Cuyahoga River, Big Creek, and Euclid Creek, resulting in vast swampy lowlands and some of the coldest winters imaginable. But proximity to all of these waterways was initially a great boon to the city. After the 1832 completion of the Ohio and Erie

Canal, which in effect linked Cleveland to the Atlantic Ocean and the Gulf of Mexico via the Mississippi, the city experienced incredible growth.

Now, even though Cleveland flourished as a midpoint in the shipping routes for the steel, oil, and coal trades in the neighboring states, it also became a manufacturing hub in its own right. To this day, the streets and buildings bear names like Carnegie and Rockefeller. The town grew by leaps and bounds after World War II, and this growth continued through the 1950s. Even its sports teams had their moments of glory, with the Indians winning the 1948 World Series and the Cleveland Browns becoming NFL champs in 1950, 1954, 1955, and 1964.

But the 1960s, a period of great turmoil throughout the United States, hit Cleveland especially hard. Major industries began to decline, and the city, which today is largely African American, was the site of major racial unrest. The white population began fleeing the city in favor of the suburbs. (Evidence of this white flight can be seen in the dates on the town welcome signs you see as you drive east on Shaker Boulevard toward Chagrin, with each successive suburb having been incorporated just after the one before it.) Factors like these resulted in a major decline in Cleveland's population, from over 914,000 in 1950 to slightly more than 570,000 in 1980. And sadly, much like Corey Haim's *E! True Hollywood Story* episode, it got worse for the Big C.

In 1969, the Cuyahoga River, a major waterway that bisects the city, caught fire. Yes, feel free to read that again: *A. River. Caught. Fire.* A small spark ignited the industrial pollutants and debris that had accumulated in a waterway so polluted that some said it "oozed rather than flowed." The fire caused major damage to two bridges. Barely a decade later, Cleveland became the first city to go into default since the Great Depression, unable to repay upwards of

$15.5 million owed mostly to six local banks. And then, in the unkindest cut of all, the sports teams truly, *truly* began to suck in whole new forms of suckiness (though the Browns *did* have some memorable years in the late '70s and in 1980). It was around this time that the sobriquet Mistake on the Lake took hold.

But hang on, Sloopy! There's still a lot of fight left in this Dawg Pound.

In 1979, voters approved an increase in the city income tax from 1% to 1.5%, and in 1980, the new mayor, George Voinovich, led an economic recovery (though the city wouldn't emerge from default until 1987) *and* also started the groundbreaking Cleveland Public-Private Partnerships to rebuild the city and restore inner-city housing as well as highways and public works. Mayor Voinovich also supported the development of the Rock and Roll

ME IN A PRODUCTION OF "THE CHOSEN"

Hall of Fame and Museum (of which I am a proud, card-carrying member) and the Great Lakes Science Center. The flagging manufacturing industry gave way to corporate headquarters, and today Cleveland is home not only to companies like the Eaton Corporation, the Sherwin-Williams Company, and KeyCorp, but also to the medical powerhouses the Cleveland Clinic and the Case Western Reserve University system of hospitals, placing it among the elite of medical research and treatment cities. The river is cleaner than ever, and tour boats course up and down the waterway. The Cleveland Play House has staged premieres for works by Tennessee Williams, Brian Friel, and William Saroyan and has featured many notable actors throughout the years, including yours truly. And sports? The Cavs had LeBron James earning back-to-back MVP honors (before he cruelly announced his departure during a prime-time TV special), the Browns are back in the NFL (after a brief, awful dismantling of the organization in the '90s), and the Tribe are playing better baseball with each successive year in one of the most beautiful ballparks around (which I will *always* call the Jake no matter what corporate teat the owners suckle).

The Cleve, the comeback kid of cities, was back—and as the Ian Hunter song, which is pretty much the unofficial city anthem and *The Drew Carey Show* opening theme, declares: Cleveland rocks!

But there is more to Cleveland than that.

Lake Erie and the surrounding rivers disperse a huge amount of moisture into Cleveland's air and soil, resulting in very warm, humid summers and frosty, massively snowy winters.

In the face of all this moisture, early settlers basically just cleared what land they needed for grazing their animals and subsistence farming. When that particular patch of earth yielded no more, they moved on. Eventually, though, the rich, moist soils by the lake blossomed with verdant orchards specializing in cherries and (if you can believe it) peaches. These were usually shipped or traded. Grape orchards followed close behind, and in fact, for a while Cuyahoga County (where Cleveland sits) was the prime producer of table grapes and even made a small amount of commercially available wine.

The Ohio and Erie Canal made shipping to the east and west easy, and grain and wheat became the crops of commerce for Ohio— and, most important, for its livestock. The soil, even at its coldest, proved to be fruitful grazing pasture, and in fact it not only launched Ohio and the Cleveland area to the fore in livestock production, but also made it a titan in the dairy industry—a fact still evident in both the local cuisine and the farmers' markets, like the phenomenal one in Shaker Square on the weekends.

Today, most of the local farming is done in the nearby areas surrounding Cleveland, and much of that is done under glass in greenhouses to protect the crops from the ravages of winter. Cleveland, developed and populated thanks to its proximity to both water and rail routes, ancient trade and immigration patterns, and nearby religious settlements, became home to diverse cultural groups, including Polish, Russian, Irish, German, Slovak, Greek, Italian, and Middle Eastern, who established their own neighborhoods. Evidence of all of these cultures can be found in the stalls of the West Side Market.

The foods most often associated with the Cleve today are generally Polish comfort staples like kielbasa and pierogi (and, well, beer) as well as a load of Hungarian and Eastern European dishes like hurka (rice sausage). The Shaker Heights area where I lived (as did Paul Newman, though not at the same time) has many authentic Hungarian restaurants offering delicious fare that will blow your taste buds away *and* insulate you like Owens Corning fiberglass insulation against the cold Cleveland winters. I'm convinced that *real* goulash could be used to make delicious adobe dwellings under the right circumstances. For real—it's as thick as a contestant on *Rock of Love.*

The unofficial official sandwich of Cleveland has got to be the Polish boy. When I saw an ad one day in the local fishwrap, *The Plain Dealer,* I laughed and said, "Ha! They're calling a po'boy a Polish boy! Ridiculous!" Overhearing this, my Cleveland-native stage manager said:

"No, dumbass. It's different. It's a Polish sausage smothered in fries, coleslaw, and really thin, sweet-spicy barbecue sauce on a bun."

"Holy shit. That sounds awesome," I said, salivating like Pavlov's pooch.

"No shit, Sherlock, it *is* awesome," he asserted through clenched teeth with a Bela Lugosi–like glare. It was amazing how instantaneously a simple joke about a sandwich—albeit the crown jewel of his city's munchables—could get his Irish up, or, in this case, his Polish. I'm convinced that if I'd made some Michael Jackson joke about him "putting a Polish boy in his mouth," he would have kicked my nuts into my throat.

And now, with the wisdom of experience, I can honestly attest that the kielbasa I had in Cleveland is some of the best sausage I have ever had. And if you go, you must try Cleveland's homemade Bertman Ball Park Mustard (it's got a red label and is hard to miss).

Nowadays the local butchers—of which there seem to be many—are using regional ingredients, like local stalwart Great Lakes Brewing Company's incredible Dortmunder Gold beer and artisanal cheeses, in their sausages to create a unique taste of the Big C. Local churches and markets alike sell fresh pierogies, which come in more varieties than the children in a Benetton ad. What is particularly cool about the Polish boy is that it's a dish made with Polish ingredients and bearing a Polish-ish (say it out loud, it's fun) name that is served *and* perfected almost exclusively at African American–owned soul-food joints! (My favorite: Hot Sauce Williams.)

Today, Cleveland's food scene shines brighter than ever before with a newly minted Iron Chef (Lola and Lolita mastermind Michael Symon) and great culinary minds-in-residence like chef and writer Michael Ruhlman. It bears noting that Cleveland was also home to the first restaurant owned and operated by another culinary titan, Italian chef Ettore "Hector" Boiardi. Now, sound out that last name . . . come on . . . that's right . . . uh-oh, SpaghettiOs, it's the man who brought spaghetti and ravioli in cans to hungry families and college stoners—not to mention millions of rations to WWII soldiers.

More recently, Cleveland culinary masterminds have created amazing farm-to-table programs, where the ingredients of many dishes originate only minutes away from the plate on which they're served, probably not unlike the experience had by the original settlers of the region, who were getting fresh dairy, meat, and produce from pastures and farms that were only a boat ride, train ride, or wagon ride away. And the prevalence of fresh, local ingredients is hardly unique to the more rarefied strata of the culinary world; there is also a formidable food scene of, by, and for the people. At the amazing Inn on Coventry, dishes like lemon-ricotta pancakes make use of the phenomenal local dairy products, and they are so good I would literally kill for some right now (really! I mean, that would be a hell of a last meal!). There are myriad soul-food joints throughout the city that have unrelentingly good fried chicken, mac and cheese, and greens and pulled pork. They even make Polish boys with pulled pork in them. It's like a pork-gasm.

There's a small, quaint strip of Mayfield Road that serves as a Little Italy, and though it is only a few blocks long, it is completely immersive: full of delicious eats, crafts, wines, and even clothing from all parts of tha Boot and deeply reflective of the proud Italian community that settled in Cleveland as far back as the Civil War. Italians had a major impact on the city's manufacturing sector, producing a diverse range of products from macaroni to cigars. It's worth noting that there was at one point a Big Italy, which was the hub of produce in town and the predecessor to the present-day Little Italy, and it was populated with tradesmen like barbers, landscapers, and stonemasons. In fact, by the 1930s, Italians in Cleveland are said to have accounted for "80% of its barbers and 70% of its cooks." By the 1960s, Italians were the second-largest European immigrant group in Cleveland.

Five Great Asian Restaurants in Cleveland

1. Siam Café
2. Superior Pho
3. Ha Ahn Korean Restaurant
4. Wonton Gourmet and BBQ
5. Li Wah

Today, there's also a thriving Asian community and a significant Chinatown that, though small by the standards of New York, San Fran, and even DC, is vibrant and full of great food, including Vietnamese, Thai, and Japanese cuisine as well as authentic Chinese fare.

☆ ☆ ☆

To observe all of these convergent cultures in action in one concentrated, conveniently located spot, there is no better destination

than Cleveland's West Side Market, one of my favorite places on earth. This teeming market had its start in 1840 and sits on the west side of the Cuyahoga River, which bisects the city. It's kind of hard not to love this place. It's a multiterminal compound that is loaded with every color, scent, and taste you can imagine. My mom still talks about her visit there, and even as the market has modernized, its rich

traditions remain, even down to the days of operation: Mondays, Wednesdays, Fridays, and Saturdays, the days on which ice was delivered back in the days before refrigeration.

Walking into the produce terminal is like running a fruit and vegetable gauntlet through two shoulder-high rows of produce with vendors shouting down to you from platforms, clamoring for your business. The experience is similar to that of walking through an Arabian marketplace, an especially apt comparison considering that the majority of the vendors are of Middle Eastern descent When I walked through the doors on the second day of my visit, gal

Remember the restaurant at the end of the aforementioned and undeniably awesome film *A Christmas Story*? Where the waiter chops the head off of the Peking duck and the waiters sing, Fa-ra-ra-ra-ra, ra-ra-ra-ra? Yup, that place was on Superior Avenue in Cleveland, and though its now closed, I am pleased to say that I did in fact eat there once. Sad to say, they used to make the unfortunate waiters reenact that scene in a kind of twisted Sino minstrel show for honkies who would squeal in khaki-clad delight at every mispronounced *l* and stroke of the cleaver, oblivious to the incredible dexterity of the same waiter who would carve delectable portions of the beheaded, ruby-skinned fowl and slip them into soft, moist rice buns using just the tip of a huge, unwieldy cleaver.

pal Erin once again in tow, I was convinced that at any moment someone would try to sell me a camel, hashish, a dagger, a genie lamp, or a nubile slave girl. As I perused the aisles, a produce vendor beckoned me over.

She: Hey! Bahama mama melon. [Offers sample.]

Me: What's that?

She: Try. Let me know. I don't know either.

Me: Where are they from?

She: From Bahama mama—Hawai'i [pronouncing it correctly, with a pause before the *ee* sound].

Me: Well, the Bahamas and Hawai'i are very different places. [I taste it. It's delish.] Mmmmmm.

She: Hey. You like it? Here's a special deal for you, my friend.

Me: Well, I don't live here, so I'm not gonna buy a melon. Why? What's the deal?

She: Well . . . you wanna talk about deal or *no deal*!

Me: No, no—tell me!

She: Cantaloupe, honeydew, and free pineapple for five dollars.

Me: Wow. That is a deal!

She: [with a "no shit" tone] Uh-huh!

Me: Well, let me think on it.

She: Honeydew, honey don't, I don't care no more!

We made a left out of the produce terminal, walked through an alleyway-type area loaded with boxes of fresh and not-so-fresh produce, and entered the main market terminal building. It truly is a Disneyland-like fantasia featuring the finest artisanal breads, exquisite desserts, and meats and cheeses from the world over.

Erin and I entered between Frank's Bratwurst (one of my mom's favorite spots—isn't she the bomb?) and a huge cheese counter. There are a disproportionate number of butchers in the market. Most have Polish, Hungarian, or Italian roots. Some counters offer meats for each community in the Cleve: hurka rice sausage, next to kielbasa (usually written "kolbasi"), next to kosher jumbos, next to Italian sausage, next to dried sausages called smokies. Most of the meat comes from Ohio farms, and a fair percentage of the poultry is from West Virginia. They also have some of the greatest turkey, chicken, and beef jerky I've ever tasted.

Some stalls and the families who run them have been in the market for decades, even 50 years or more. These are people with longtime, multigenerational roots in Ohio, and in this market it's not uncommon to encounter people (generally older) speaking Polish, Italian, or Hungarian or wearing traditional Hungarian or Mennonite clothing. There is some competition among vendors, as many of their goods overlap. A young lady who works at a stand

whose stuffed olives are some of the greatest on earth confided that her neighbors, supposedly a dairy stand, were suddenly selling olives and marinated veggies even though they were not supposed to. But the cream always rises to the top, and this hardworking olive lady had just finished stuffing 80 pounds' worth right behind the counter.

The other thing that is so cool about the market is that it really reflects regional—as opposed to ethnic—taste buds. I watched an African American woman in her 30s order some souse meat, a pressed meat terrine loaf similar to headcheese but pickled with vinegar. The slices look like a carnivore's stained glass window, with meat bits floating in sliced meat. I asked her what was in it. She replied, "Pig parts." Yum. (I later found out that the ingredients are pork, pork skin, pork snout, water, vinegar, and pork tongue.) I asked if it was good. "Well," she replied, "I know mah dude like it, so I get it for him. 'Sgood with saltine crackers." Perhaps it is, I thought—but I shall never know.

Now, even if you don't get a brat, or one of the amazing gyro sandwiches with orange, garlicky, sour cream–based tzatziki sauce, or the great falafel from the neatly tucked-away Maha café, you can easily eat your way from one end of the market to the other just on the free samples you're given by the vendors, who are fiercely proud of their wares. Everything from delicious, award-winning Dichotomy Corn (a Cheddar-caramel hybrid popcorn) to the formidable yet miniscule Oooooooh . . . FUDGE stand, where owner/chef/proprietor Sam makes fudges in flavors like horchata and orange Creamsicle plus chocolate truffles flavored with everything from bacon to raspberry and chipotle to gold dust. And in many cases,

merely striking up a conversation with these vendors, who are some of the nicest people on earth, will yield not only free samples, but also free wares—which is, needless to say, extraordinarily cool.

This particular day, I wanted to try something from a creperie in the far southwest corner of the building. Crepes have never been a go-to food for me, so I went with the owner's suggestion, the Montreal: smoked brisket and Emmenthal (a Swiss-like) cheese. All of his ingredients were from Ohio, many were from other vendors in the market, and all were preservative free.  We grabbed a seat on the balcony overlooking the market and sat down to chow. Though hardly a connoisseur, I have to say that it was by far the single greatest crepe I have ever eaten, slightly crispy at the edges, chewy in the center, cheesy, slightly smoky, and salty, but perfect in every way.

Having feasted with both my mouth and eyes, I was now thirsty, so Erin and I headed down the street to what just might be my favorite brewery in the United States, the Great Lakes Brewing Company.

Now, while this time-honored company has a massive following and I myself have put a hurt on several bottles of their *amazing* Dortmunder Gold and *phenomenal* Christmas Ale, during my time in Cleveland I hadn't been to the brewery itself. It's a massive brick structure on Carroll at 26th Street, just down the street from the West Side Market, and its tasting room complex houses a bar, a restaurant, a gift shop, and even an entertainment venue. Today, however, I wanted to see the epicenter, the actual beer works.

Erin and I walked to a nondescript door on the side of the building and knocked, noting with disappointment that the last tour had apparently ended just 20 minutes before we arrived. Damn! I was never to have my *Laverne and Shirley* moment, looking on wistfully as the bottles scuttled past on the processing line. Before we could turn to leave, two gentlemen came to the door, one a slim, bespectacled dude who looked like the cool teacher who inspires you to learn physics, the other a younger fella in a ball cap. We explained that we'd been hoping for a tour, especially since I was leaving the next day, but saw that they'd ended. They must have seen the heartbreak in my face because the guy in the glasses said, "Aw, heck, come on—I'll give you a tour!" I was so revved up that Erin had to touch my arm and say, "Okay, okay, calm down."

I asked the cool gent who'd granted us our tour what his name was.

"Pat," he replied.

"Oh, and you run the tours?"

"Oh, no. I'm the owner." *The owner???* The co-owner, Patrick Conway, was giving two random-ass, unannounced strangers a tour? After hours? That is the type of stuff that makes me love Cleveland and its salt-of-the-earth, deeply cool people. We walked around to the loading dock, past a white van labeled Fatty Wagon. I asked Pat about the moniker.

"We take the grease from the restaurant's deep fryer, heat it, filter it, decant it, and when it cools, we use it to run our trucks."

Say what? Great beer and social conscious-  ness? I nearly kissed him. He explained as we entered the brewery itself that it had been the stables for the now-defunct Schlather brewery, which had operated across the street eons before. In fact, the hayloft above the brewery floor had deposited so much hay into the ceiling that they use it as insulation to this day, and not only in the brewery. The outer wall of their beer garden is insulated with nothing more than hay bales and stucco.

They also happen to heat the place with a system of hot-water pipes that run beneath the floor and a small, igneous rock fireplace fueled by "logs" made from the cardboard cores of discarded plastic shrink-wrap rolls that are stuffed with cinnamon sticks. To quote Pat, between trucks running on fryer grease and the fireplace, "We've taken two waste streams and made a fuel out of them." This place, much like Cleveland, rocks.

He guided me through the plant, which managed to give off a homey impression despite its size. He showed me the different hops and grains that go into each variety of their incredible beer, all of which have the coolest names around, including Nosferatu, Commodore Perry, Eliot Ness, Burning River, Dortmunder Gold, and the almost impossible to get Christmas Ale, nearly cracklike in its addictive nature.

I especially love that they honor those who were there before them, even preserving the Schlather plant's original stone signage, which can be viewed on their tour.

Pat is without doubt an amazing dude insofar as his social consciousness and environmental views go, but I would be remiss if I did not mention that this man, and indeed all of those in his employ, is a straight-up beer pimp with impressive knowledge

The famed Dortmunder Gold beer, the Great Lakes Brewing Company's first beer and first award-winning beer, was first called the Heisman. It was named for the famed football player who loaned his name to the college trophy—and happened to live around the corner from the brewery.

culled directly from visits to European microbreweries and from master brewer Thaine Johnson, whose 40 years of experience includes managing Cleveland's Christian Schmidt Brewery (which was the 10th-largest brewery in the country in the late 1970s, but closed in the mid-1980s) and who joined Great Lakes during the company's earliest days. Even the yeast starters, or primers, that are the foundations of any good beer are truly authentic. The ale yeast primer comes from England, the pilsner from Czechoslovakia. But the taste is strictly their own. As Pat explained, "You can train yeast by temperatures. When you run a yeast through your own little 'program,' you can get certain flavors out of the yeast during fermentation." They use no preservatives and never pasteurize. This place turns out rich, chocolatey porters and crisp ales, hoppy ambers and . . . well, you get the gist—great freakin' beer.

Pat walked me through the process of making the beers and showed me the inside of the massive, towering mash tanks. Mashing is the mixing of barley and water to break down the starches into sugars. Once the sugars are released, the soggy barley is usually discarded. Great Lakes, on the other hand, spreads it on screen racks in the building's earthen basement. They bring in red wiggler worms to eat the barley, and some of their castings (also known as worm dookie) are given to Amish farmers to use as a

> Not only is worm poop an incredible and virtually odorless fertilizer, but the worms also aerate the soil, earning them the nickname the intestines of the earth.

formidable fertilizer or used on GLB's own farm—yes, a brewery with its own land.

And check this coolness out. Not only does Great Lakes grow *all* the produce and herbs that are served in its restaurant, but the farm also is part of a 19th-century village run by the Western Reserve Historical Society, which Pat awesomely described as "you know, those people walking around in period outfits talking about history." And they farm using the methods of the 19th century, with no pesticides or herbicides. Any remaining soggy barley is used in Great Lakes' restaurant's breads and pretzels!

The restaurant itself is on Market Street in two 19th-century Victorian buildings, the Market Tavern and MacClean's Feed and Seed Company, that have been fused into one kick-ass plant. The space houses a performance venue and drinkery in the cellar, a beer garden, and a pub. The pub is exactly what you'd want and expect from a place with so much warmth, integrity, and history: high tables, warm lighting, and a dark wooden bar with .38-caliber bullet holes allegedly put there by the one-time Cleveland director of public safety, the "Untouchable" Eliot Ness.

Pat introduced me to his chef, who brought out what I consider to be two of the greatest dishes to ever accompany beer: their homemade pretzels with an amazing mustard and liptauer cheese dip (a Hungarian specialty), and pierogies with grilled kolbasi. The pierogies were crispy at the edges and buttery pillow-soft and chewy in the center, and the sausage was amazingly flavorful and perfectly cooked. The barley-laden pretzels were the perfect accompaniment to the beer that shared their barley pedigree, especially when accompanied by the creamy cheese dip.

Pretzels, cheese, sausage, pierogies, Great Lakes' delicious beer (Christmas Ale that day), good friends, good people, and good times. I even had my *Laverne and Shirley* moment. Those reasons and

many more are why I reject any talk of mistakes on lakes. It's a town of good honest
flavors and good honest people, and if you
let her, Cleveland will open her orange-
and-brown-clad arms and embrace you
with kisses of Parma and pierogies, kol-

basi and kettle corn, brats, beer, and a hearty laugh, hug, and pat
on the back. Cleveland, land of Indians and industry. The time-
worn, weathered, wonderful underdog city still has a vibrant heart
that pumps with all of the flavors and history of those who have
crossed her borders, chanted in her Dawg Pound, toiled in her
foundries, and worked her docks. It's a city with the soul of a town,
and it's coming back better than ever.

And you know that beautiful stadium at the corner of Carnegie
and Ninth? The one with a great, albeit struggling, ball club that
calls its players Pronk and Jhonny and its mascot Wahoo? Well, no
offense to Progressive, which now owns the naming rights to the
field, but I still call it the Jake. And Cleveland wouldn't have it any
other way.

Cleveland rocks, and the only Mistake on the Lake is the one
you make by not going to check it out for yourself. It tastes of garlic,
great beer, bratwurst, and brown bread; sounds like rock 'n' roll and
railroads; and continues to wrestle with the mystery of its history.

Hungarian Liptauer Cheese Spread

Makes 1¾ cups

This goes well with beer. Serve it with pumpernickel or rye bread.

If you cannot find Liptauer cheese (better known as Lipto), you can substitute an equal amount of cream cheese or feta.

2 anchovy fillets

8 ounces Liptauer cheese

½ cup butter, softened

3 tablespoons thick sour cream

1 teaspoon capers (optional)

1 tablespoon finely chopped onion

1 tablespoon mustard

1½ teaspoons paprika + additional for garnish

½ teaspoon caraway seeds, smashed or bruised to release flavor

½ teaspoon salt

Fresh parsley

Place the anchovies in a bowl and pound with a wooden spoon or pestle until well mashed. Add the cheese, butter, sour cream, and capers (if using), and blend thoroughly. Stir in the onion, mustard, paprika, caraway seeds, and salt. Combine the ingredients thoroughly. Cover and refrigerate for at least 2 hours to blend the flavors.

Serve the cheese mixture mounded on a plate and sprinkle with paprika and fresh parsley.

CHAPTER 6

✮ ✮ ✮

HALLOWEEN WEEKEND, 2009

Or: The Freaks

Come Out at Night

✮ ✮ ✮

AUSTIN, TX

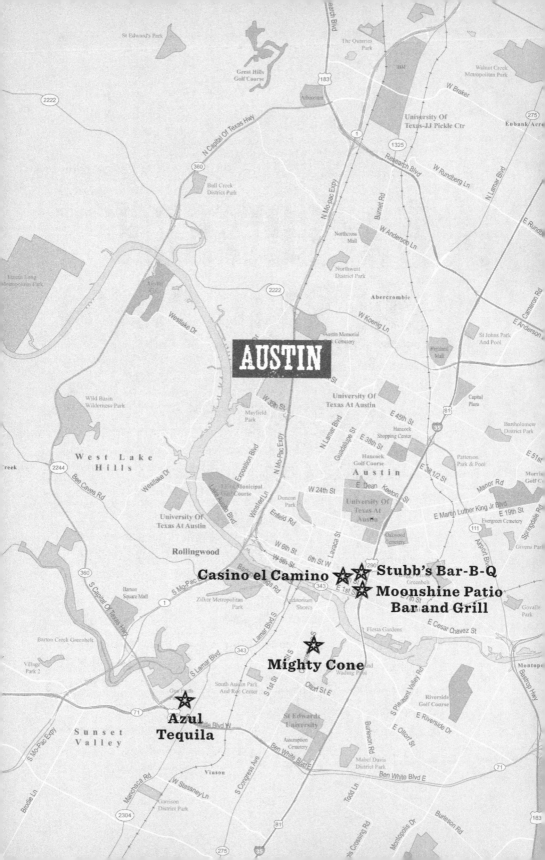

AUSTIN

Casino el Camino ☆ ☆ Stubb's Bar-B-Q

☆ Moonshine Patio Bar and Grill

☆ Mighty Cone

☆ Azul Tequila

The celebration of Halloween in Austin rivals that of Mardi Gras in New Orleans in size, scope, and utter abandon. I'd fallen deeply, madly in love with Austin on prior trips, but I knew that I'd never truly know her until I had joined in on the festivities at one of the best times of the year to be there. So, I booked my ticket, packed my bags, and prepared to have an incredible Halloween in the place that prides itself on "keeping it weird."

I met my friend Danielle, a former Austinite, in Houston and we drove together to Austin, ready for a great weekend. First I had to navigate the city's screwed-up highways and streets. In Austin it's hard to tell when you're getting on the highway, when you're off, what's a one-way and what isn't—urban legend has it that the man who laid out the streets of the city saw what he'd created and committed suicide. Arriving at my destination felt like I had passed some unspoken test to prove myself worthy of the bountiful treasures I had come to consume.

I saw the first signs of Halloweird the moment I walked into my hotel's lobby. The front desk clerk had flames drawn on her head and neck and a tiny stuffed dragon perched on her shoulder. "I'm a maiden sacrificed to a dragon!" she announced. Of course you are, dear. Then a drunken Borat stumbled into the lobby arm in arm with a naughty (read: slutty) version of the oft-dreamed-of-genie Jeannie and Batman, all three very happy and even more intoxicated, singing the Human League's "Don't You Want Me." And Halloween was still two days away. Ah yes, Austin, you never fail to make me smile. And yes, you are weird.

After a late start the following day, I was ready to get the weekend started and have my first big meal. After some back-and-forth with Danielle, we decided on a hidden jewel—and I do not use this term as some precious little wank. This place is hidden, precious, and it glows. Its name is Azul Tequila.

Located in a strip mall near Lamar and Ben White, this little establishment has garnered a reputation for great Mexican food in a town where that is not a distinction to be conferred lightly. After failing to find it on our own even after a few frustrating calls to the hostess, Sergio Varela, a co-owner, guided us in himself like an air traffic controller coaching the passenger who has taken over for the sick pilot in an action film. I mean, it's a really busy place and he all but parked my car for me. Austin, *te amo*.

We walked into a place longer than it was wide and awash in paint of every jewel-tone color you can imagine. It's like a tortilla factory run by Willy Wonka, but in a good way. We were hit immediately with the smell of spices: not just the typical chile perfume so commonly found in places with Aztec masks and sombreros on the wall, but unexpected smells like cinnamon and clove. The mariachi band, six pieces strong, was playing—I shit you not—"Who Let the Dogs Out?" (Who? Who? Who?) and absolutely killing it. Austin is after all, the live music capital of America.

Danielle and I sat on a comfy banquette and were promptly given menus. Some things I recognized but plenty I didn't, and even the familiar recipes seemed to be prepared with a different approach. I wanted to simply say, "Yes." Now, Danielle is a bona fide foodie with an appetite that equals and at times bests my own, even though she's less than half my size. Together we usually do two appetizers, two entrées, and one other something, and we share the lot. But we were having trouble limiting our order to just five dishes.

Our very sweet albeit English-deficient waitress sort of pointed us through the menu and guided our choices. For our apps, we went with queso compuesto—melted cheese mixed with poblano chile, tomatoes, ground beef, and guacamole (another very famous version of this layered cheese dip in Austin is made by the Magnolia Café, where it's called Mag Mud)—and pozole Mexiquense, red hominy soup with chunks of pork served with lettuce, radish, onions, avocado, and oregano—that's served only on weekends.

For entrées we chose two dishes, both legendary at Azul Tequila and examples of the South-Central Mexican cuisine Sergio has become known for. The cochinita pibil is a spicy Mayan version of pork barbacoa. The meat for this dish is usually cut from the head of a pig (or a cow for the beef version), marinated with achiote sauce, cooked in banana leaves, and served with pickled onions, habanero peppers, plantains, and black beans. Our other entrée was pescado empapelado, a flaky white fish fillet (probably tilapia) cooked with chipotle sauce while wrapped in foil—presumably to steam it and to further deepen the spices and flavor of the fish. It was served with avocado salad and black beans.

Now, me ordering slow-cooked spicy pork at a good Mexican restaurant is a no-brainer, but up until this point I had never once ordered fish. Danielle, though, sold me on it by simply saying, "Mexican fish dishes are amazing, and if you're gonna get one, here would be the place." Our waitress recommended the empapelado.

But after ordering, I felt a deep regret. I couldn't eat at one of Austin's best Mexican restaurants without ordering something made with nopales, or cactus paddles. Danielle suggested that I just order a side of nopales, a great idea that further affirmed my belief that women are smarter than men.

Two shots of tequila later, the music still phenomenal, our first wave of food arrived. The queso was delicious and a far cry from the glowing radioactive yellow sludge I was used to—and it bears noting

WORLD'S BEST HANGOVER
CURE, POZOLE

that if you add avocado to *anything,* I will likely eat it or make love to it—or both. The pozole was a meal unto itself.

With cubes of melt-in-your-mouth pork the size of children's blocks (let's pause while I try to calm myself) and tender, marble-size pieces of hominy (corn kernels treated with an alkali, like lye, to make them supple), the pozole alone made the trip to Azul Tequila worth it. What was absolutely amazing about getting these two dishes to start off with was that they immediately showcased not only the range of Azul Tequila's menu, but also the diverse range of culinary influences in Austin, the queso compuesto being unquestionably Tex-Mex and the pozole representing what Sergio refers to as Mexican Interior cuisine, the cuisine of South-Central Mexico.

The nopales were just about the coolest, weirdest things ever (though it should be noted that they are best appreciated in small doses). Glistening with oil from the pan, they were plump, succulent ovals about the size of Ping-Pong paddles. They had a juicy, almost slimy mouthfeel similar to okra with the moist chewiness of zucchini.

As we waited for our entrées, Sergio came over to our table. His first question was what had we ordered, but before I could answer he said, "You got the chile relleno, right?"

I said, "Nope. The cochinita pibil and the empapelado."

"Okay, but you got the cabrito, right?"

"No. I tried it in San Antonio once and it was all fatty, stringy, and gross. Not my thing."

He looked at me as though I'd told him I'd never seen the sun.

"Okay," he said. We talked briefly about the restaurant and the type of food he serves. He explained that these dishes came from his childhood home, a small town in Tejupilco. This little town is surrounded by the states of Mexico, Michoacan, and Guerrero. He said what makes his town's cuisine so unique is that it is, like Austin is in Texas, a central hub in Mexico that draws on the influences of the states around it. They have pork dishes, but they also get fish from traders going inland. They have beef dishes, but they also have goats from nearby farms where the grazing is more conducive to feeding them than cows. Perhaps most important was that these recipes are literally the stuff he grew up on and came directly from his mom. Some were dishes for special occasions like birthdays and weddings, and others were hangover cures for his dad. After hearing this amazing explanation of the journey I was about to take, I mentioned how much I was enjoying the mariachi band and that I'd sung the mariachi staple "Arboles de la Barranca" in a show back at Yale. He laughed at this stocky Jew claiming to have wielded a guitarrón and big sombrero while wearing *very* tight pants (I admit it is a funny visual), then disappeared with a mischievous smile.

When Danielle and I had gotten to the bottom of the queso and had put a hurt on the pozole, we ordered two more chilled shots of silver tequila—lovely, cold, tangy, and lethal. Then the main event, the entrées, arrived.

The cochinita pibil was just beautiful to behold. Bright red in color—most likely from the achiote—it looked like pulled pork but with larger chunks and virtually no fat. It was served atop five long, flat strips of plantain, splayed out like a pale yellow hand, which were arranged atop a banana leaf (a key ingredient in the dish). Alongside were a bowl of silky black beans with a beautiful,

Achiote spice is made from the seeds in the inedible fruit of the annatto tree or bush. The seeds also are often used as a coloring additive or ground into a paste to be used for both flavor and color. It's a great alternative to saffron, which is, like, mega-expensive—at the writing of this book, the cheapest stuff is going for $150 an ounce!

almost purple shimmer and a red tortilla cup of bright pink pickled onions.

The empapelado fish was brought to the table in a pouch of aluminum foil—a stark contrast to the sheer beauty of the cochinita's presentation—with a simple avocado salad and rice riding shotgun.

Like I said, I had not typically indulged in fish at Mexican restaurants. This dish changed that forever. When I rolled back the aluminum foil covering, a steam cloud of spice and chipotle cooked into a harmonious blend with the fish rolled toward my shnozola and made my head spin. But as delectable as the smell was, I can only describe what hit my tongue as a revelation, a smoky caramel in both taste and texture. The natural butteriness of the fish coupled with the velvety texture of the chipotle sauce to meld into a texture not unlike custard. Just remarkable. And then, believe it or not, the meal got even more incredible.

A waiter I had not seen before came over with a stack of tortilla containers, explaining that they held homemade white corn tortillas, and then he said, "Sergio wants you to try the cabrito and the relleno." Before I could say, "No *guey*," two more glorious plates of

Maguey is a succulent plant, "though not a cactus," and a member of the agave family. The leaves contain a lot of sap, which makes them good eating. The stalks are roasted and can be chewed and sucked on like sugarcane.

Guajillo is a mildly spicy pepper of only about 2,500 to 5,000 Scoville units. It is often dried and made into a flavoring paste.

Poblano peppers take their name from the region they come from, Puebla, Mexico. They are very mild in flavor, not unlike bell peppers. Their large size makes them ideal for stuffing.

South-Central Mexico's finest were brought to our already brimming table.

Cabrito al maguey is South-Central Mexican barbacoa-style goat meat that is marinated with guajillo chiles and slow cooked on maguey leaves. It had a pulled pork visual aesthetic but a deep, rich, chocolate color. It arrived at our table with wedges of lime; charro beans in a clear, savory broth; and some of the most fragrant and visually pleasing salsa verde I have ever seen.

The chile relleno en crema was a poblano pepper as large as a size 7 sneaker stuffed with a mixture of sautéed pork, almonds, raisins (yes, raisins!), tomatoes, and onions. It was topped with a velvety white tomato cream sauce and sprinkled with toasted slivered almonds (an ingredient I am not at all used to seeing in Mexican cuisine, let alone in a chile relleno). The relleno, it bears mentioning, has never been one of my favorite dishes, largely because green peppers usually just don't sit all that well with me and I'm not super-fond of their flavor. But this dish was truly unlike any version I have ever seen, and I loved it instantly. I apparently took three bites in a row with my eyes closed. It was orgasmic. Seriously. I'm seeking help for this.

And then the mariachi band appeared table-side.

Boom.

Clad in white and brown regalia, the musicians all shouted hello and said, "We hear you have a favorite song, and maybe . . . you sing it with us?" Danielle burst out laughing. She had heard me claim to have been a mariachi when we were talking to Sergio, but I think she was as shocked as I was that they were call-

> Great Food Songs
>
> Jambalaya (on the Bayou)—Hank Williams
> Cheeseburger in Paradise—Jimmy Buffett
> Chicken Soup with Rice—Carole King
> Food, Glorious Food—*Oliver!* soundtrack
> Cold Beverage—G Love and Special Sauce
> Home Cookin'—Junior Walker and the All-Stars
> Texas Cookin'—George Strait
> Mama's Fried Chicken—Roddie Romero and the Hub City All-Stars
> Smokey Joe's Barbecue—Johnny Horton
> Cherry Lime Rickey—Krayo (from Iller than Theirs)

ing my bluff. But I was not going to be punked. I hopped out of the booth, turned to the assembled band, and said, "'Arboles de la Barranca,' boys, A minor."

And these guys just dropped the hammer. I mean, just the most glorious sound. I bounced with the music and then, with grand, sweeping arm gestures, I regaled the audience about the "Trees in the Valley"—in Spanish. The guys were shocked that I knew the words, and that I could carry a tune. To be honest, so was I. And to be completely honest, the tequila helped.

The song done, I tipped the band and thanked them, warning them that my food was getting cold and they risked severe bodily harm by keeping me from the task at hand, just in case they had any ideas about an encore.

I sat down and grabbed a tortilla from the stack we'd been brought. Now, in the age-old corn versus flour debate, I always tend to go with flour because though I love the taste of corn I am not fond of the slightly coarse, crumbly mouthfeel. Well, these homemade white corn tortillas were the absolute perfect hybrid, the Tortilla Prius, if you will. All the great aroma and taste of corn with the softness and tear of flour. I scooped up some of the tender goat meat, added some of the charro beans and a little raw white onion, and bit into pure deliciousness. The tenderness, the hint of gaminess, the small hit of heat from the guajillo, the crunch of the white onion, and the pillowy softness of the charro beans were in perfect harmony—unlike me and the mariachis. It was a meal made by a family, fit for a king, and served up in a strip mall in Austin.

As we left, or, I should say, waddled out of, the restaurant, Danielle and I could hear peals of laughter, screaming, and hollering in the distance. We looked at our watches. It was past midnight. It was Halloween in Austin. Duck and cover. Back to the hotel and ready to start anew on All Hallow's Eve.

Before you read any further, I must make one thing clear about Austin, Texas.

I fucking love Austin, Texas.

Love it.

Love it like a beautiful woman with an ample bosom, carrying delicious food and a cold beer, with whom I run through fields at the end of the movie, laughing and joining hands and swinging around in circles as the music swells . . . and then as the sun sets over the Texas Hill Country, we drink, eat, make love, and listen to Stevie Ray Vaughan's cover of Jimi Hendrix's "Little Wing." And truth be told, in Austin I *have* eaten like a king, drunk like a fish, sworn like a sailor, partied like a rock star, and made love like Dionysus, all while watching the sun set over the Hill Country and listening to Stevie Ray. It is dreams made manifest, and it is by far one of my favorite places on planet Earth. Hook 'em, Horns. (I didn't go to the University of Texas and have never even attended a game, but my love of Austin—and certain UT grads—has me raising my pointer and pinkie in Longhorn solidarity. Holla.)

I mention my partiality for Austin not as an excuse or as a disclaimer, just as a statement of fact. You should simply know that while I will absolutely give you the straight dope on ATX, it's coming through the filter of a dude who would marry that city without a pre-nup after only three dates.

As cities go, Austin is a lovely, weird paradox.

One would think that in a state that has given us some of our most ardent conservative, right-wing politicians, policies, and presidents, as well as people who love them, the capital city would be the epicenter, the shining example of the conservative ideal. Well, it didn't go down like that. Austin, named for the state paterfamilias, Stephen F. Austin, is as I mentioned known as the Live Music Capital, which you have to admit is a really cool distinction. It is anything but a conservative city. As the one blue spot in a red state, Austin's identity is defiantly liberal-minded; witness its motto: "Keep Austin Weird." And it does: The city has naked swimmin' holes! Matt McConaughey plays the bongos naked! Bats hang from underpasses!

The city is equally devoted to keeping it green. Austin, voted one of the 10 greenest cities in America by MSN in 2007, puts forth considerable effort to minimize its carbon footprint and to invest in green technologies to preserve the awesomeness of ATX for years to come. These efforts by the municipal government are reflected in the attitudes of the business community and the city's residents. This isn't some new trend they're jumping on; this mind-set has been around nearly as long as the city itself. The relationship with the land goes back to when the streets had no names, and it truly runs that deep.

And the food? Oh my, oh my, oh my . . .

Insanely delicious food, influenced by the strangest hodgepodge of culture collisions found smack-dab (clap-clap-clap-clap) deep in the heart of Texas. So how did this juxtaposition of red and blue,

Word to the wise to those visiting: Austinites *do not* pronounce Guadalupe Street Wah-dah-lou-pay or Gwah-dah-lou-pay. Its Gwah-dah-loop. Thank me later.

conservative and liberal, weird and, well, just plain weird come to pass? How does it all reconcile?

First off, to understand Austin, or any city in the state of Texas for that matter, you need to understand where it lies geographically in terms of rivers, proximity to the coast, and neighbors on all sides. When you realize that this one state is larger than the entire nation of France or California and second only to Alaska in the United States, you understand that you're dealing with a lot of land and a *lot* of variables. The landscape changes dramatically as you travel across the vast expanse of the Lone Star State. Working your way from east to west, as I did on my first solo cross-country drive (undertaken after a monster-ass breakup—there are few better therapies than getting away from all you know in this fashion), you see woods and swampland give way to vast stretches of plain and prairie with oceans of blowing grass. Eventually you hit the desert and rocky, rugged mountains that most people associate with Texas. In fact, less than 10% of Texas is desert, and most of its major cities are close to the coast, springs, or verdant grasslands and rivers.

Now, because of where Austin is situated, in the center of the state atop the Balcones Fault Zone, it lays claim to all the terrains and topsoils of Texas, not to mention some incredible geologic formations.

Sometimes these formations are aboveground, as in the case of Pilot Knob, and in other places there are natural springs like San Pedro Springs, San Marcos Springs, and Barton Springs. These pools provide freshwater, are ridiculous amounts of fun to swim in, and were a natural attraction for settlers. There is actually evidence that prehistoric humans lived in the Balcones region of Texas 11,000 years ago.

Aside from the Balcones Fault, Austin is also bordered by the Colorado River (not to be confused with the famous one that runs

A quick primer for those of you who may have been daydreaming during earth science class: A fault is a fracture in the bedrock where the rock on either side has moved parallel to the fracture. It's like placing triangular blocks together to form a square and then sliding one up, down, or alongside the other. Sweet visual, huh? (Thanks are due to my environmental science teacher, Mr. Zinn—who was a little prick but a knowledgeable one—and to my folks for buying me triangular blocks.) In Austin, the fault line actually runs more or less along the route of the MoPac Expressway.

from Colorado into the Sea of Cortez), which brings with it mineral deposits and currents to aid in the generation of hydroelectric power. As I said, Texas's landscape changes drastically from east to west, and from north to south as well. Because Austin is smack-dab (clap-clap-clap-clap) deep in the heart of Texas, it's at the intersection of four major ecological environs. It's part green oasis, part desert, part tropics, and part wetlands. All this varied topography supports great biological and agricultural diversity.

So we know the land, but what about those who live off of it? It is impossible to talk about Texas without acknowledging neighboring Mexico, both as a shaper of its history and as a key component of its cultural and demographic landscapes.

While visiting ATX to film an episode of my show, I had the chance to sit down for a few beers with some successful local business owners of Mexican descent. They'd all known each other for years, and each was influential in the city. I was hoping to get from them a sense of Austin's history, how it became such a cool, diverse place. They showed me pictures of their times growing up both in Mexico and in Texas.

"There's a renaissance happening in Austin, man!" said a big round man in his 50s who looked not unlike Mario from the Nintendo games and like James Earl Jones would sound with a Mexican accent. "A real one! Not Texan, not Mexican. Like a . . . " He interlaced his fingers, "It's all together now, bro. It's all Austin, you know?"

Before ever going to Austin, I had read that it was an early hub of Tex-Mex cuisine. But though I'd seen this ubiquitous term on countless frozen entrées and shopping mall food court menus, I didn't actually know what it connoted. It might just as well have been the birthplace of Sasquatch for all that catchall phrase conveyed. (And having now spent a Halloween in Austin, I can say fairly confidently that I have seen the big, hairy bastard making out with a UT co-ed on Sixth Street with a bottle of Lone Star in one paw and what might have been a deer carcass in the other. Then again, I had been drinking. Don't judge. It's Austin. Keep it weird. Moving on . . .)

The term actually refers to a railroad company, the Texas Mexican. Train schedules of the 1800s abbreviated the names of railroads, making the Missouri Pacific the MoPac (which lends its name to the Loop 1 freeway in Austin to this day) and the Texas Mexican the TexMex. In the 1920s, newspapers like Ohio's *Newark Advocate* and North Carolina's *Gastonia Daily Gazette* used "Tex-Mex" to refer to people of Mexican descent who were born in Texas. But there is actually a far more accurate term to describe those people and the culture they spawned in the Rio Grande region and in Austin: Tejano. It's a word that can refer to a type of music or even to a style of dress, but that is just the tip of the iceberg. The term gets to the heart of the food, soul, music, and culture that make up Austin's charm, appeal, and allure.

In Spanish, *"tejano"* simply refers to someone from Texas, regardless of race or ethnic background, and while the term is generally associated with those of Spanish Texan descent (Texas was part of New Spain until Mexico gained its independence in 1821, from which Texas went on to gain its independence in 1836), it also encompasses a surprising number of races and ethnicities that had footholds in the Lone Star State. This is important because those who settled in and around Austin were actually closer to the Spanish culturally than to Mexicans, who identified more with mestizo Central Mexican culture. But "Hispanicized" peoples of other cultures, most of whom entered the mix as part of Spain's colonial expansion, were considered Tejanos as well. People of Filipino, French, Italian, Polish, Czech, Swedish, Danish, Dutch, Irish, Scottish, Welsh, African, and even Arab descent settled in Texas from colonial times through the Mexican Revolution, and *all* were considered Tejanos. And even my people, the Jews, settled there when they fled the Inquisition, and they too were considered Tejanos. "Ich bin ein Tejano!"

Today, Tejanos are mostly white Hispanics and can be Spanish or Mexican in ancestral heritage, though most are of Mexican American descent. But today's Tejanos and the food they put forth echo the influences of *all* the cultures that came before them. So, just as Tex-Mex was once a less apt descriptor of the people of Texas than Tejano was, the cuisine that is often called Tex-Mex would more accurately be called Tejano, as it represents this mix of influences as much as the people, and for that matter, the city of Austin.

All those cultures and all those soils and all that different terrain and vegetation make Austin's culinary profile like a greatest-hits record of Texas's food. It's literally the personification of everything that makes the state and country great, and hey, with apologies to John Mellencamp, ain't that America?

We got a late start the next day. Brunch time had passed, but I had to venture out in search of more deliciousness, so onward we went to Moonshine Patio Bar and Grill, the recommendation of another friend and Austin native. We pulled up to the old stone building on Red River Street in the heart of downtown.

I was wearing my Yankee cap, and as the Yanks were in the World Series (which they would eventually win), I high-fived the dude in the A-Rod jersey I passed on my way up the stairs to the enclosed porch. The building is part of the Waterloo Compound, a collection of some of the oldest commercial buildings in all of Austin. The restaurant itself was once the Sunday House—a small building used as a warehouse—of a German settler and freighter named Henry Hofheintz.

The building housing Moonshine is more than 150 years old and still has the original cedar posts, limestone walls, and ceiling beams. Danielle and I sat at a corner table by the window with the warm Texas sun streaming through it and were given old Ball canning jars full of water (an homage to the moonshine liquor they would have held back in the day). We ordered drinks—an Ann's Bloody Mary with chipotle, olive, and garlic for Danielle and a Hard Lemonade with vodka, mint, fresh lemonade, and Paula's Texas Lemon for me—and sat back to contemplate the menu.

Moonshine characterizes its cuisine as "an innovative take on classic American comfort food" that will satisfy "even big city tastes," and I worried that I might be faced with the shit that drives me crazy back in New York, like chefs who take highbrow ingredients "slumming" to come up with a $95 foie gras cheeseburger. Not so at Moonshine. These guys elevate simple dishes, and do it *perfectly*.

We ordered roasted garlic bulbs with goat cheese, roasted red peppers, and toast points, which was exactly what it sounds like but flawlessly executed, the roasted garlic spreading like cream on the toast. We had to order the deviled crab backs with crawfish crabmeat stuffing and Tabasco butter just because I thought it sounded like pure sex, and was I ever right. These things were gloriously overstuffed orange, red, and yellow diamonds. The stuffing consistency was somewhere between traditional turkey dressing and quiche, and the Tabasco butter added just the right amount of vinegary heat. I could have rocked two orders myself, but by this point the chef had recognized me from my show and was insisting that I

When the German immigrants who settled the rural areas around Austin and the neighboring cities of New Braunfels and Fredericksburg needed to shop at Austins markets and attend church on Sundays, storehouse owners like the Hofheintz family would clear their Sunday Houses of goods to accommodate them on Saturday night. This enabled the visitors to take care of their commercial and religious needs on Sunday before returning home. Moonshine occupies the last Sunday House still standing in Austin.

try one of their signature dishes, the Moonshine "Corn Dog" Shrimp. How could I say
no? The fat, skewered shrimp were encased
in crispy, sweet corn dog batter and served
with one of the greatest condiments man-
kind has ever seen: homemade honey and

blueberry mustard swirled together. Together, the combination provides multiple levels of sweetness, between the honey, the blueberry,
and the cornmeal. Major success.

My "big city tastes" remained very happy through my rainbow trout stuffed with corn bread and chile butter, and Danielle
was just as pleased with her buffalo meatloaf with mushroom
gravy, a real frontier dish. Even the bread-crumb-crusted mac
and pimento cheese (you read that right) and *ridonkulously
perfectly* roasted sweet potatoes were stellar examples of simple
ingredients crafted masterfully. Perhaps best of all was a roasted
corn relish that truly had all the elements and flaws of chuck
wagon frontier cooking. It is a travesty that this got a mention
only as a "seasonal vegetable" on the menu.

The chef, James "Hoss" Bowen, was a
mountain of a man, all ovals and spheres
with bright blue eyes and a smile that shone
like an Austin moontower (the 165-foot-tall
carbon arc streetlights Austin erected in the
1890s, some of which still stand today).

He insisted that we try dessert, and my
Lord am I glad I did. I swear on all things I hold sacred that the
peanut butter mousse pie was the absolute best peanut butter dessert I have ever tasted, with a texture that hovered between cheesecake and mousse—and somewhere between here and heaven. At

Hoss's urging I paired it with a Guinness stout, and the combination of pie and rich stout may be the death-row final bite. The other dessert was representative of the German and Dutch heritage that is so prevalent in Austin and Central Texas, an apple pie served in a skillet and topped with homemade maple ice cream. Fruit desserts aren't usually my thing, so factor that in when I tell you that I nearly made love to this pie with my face. All in all, such a decadent meal that I had to unbutton my vest and go for a very long constitutional (though I could have walked to Guam and not mitigated the caloric intake at that meal). As we strolled, Lion-O and the Thundercats danced by along with Hunter S. Thompson, the Bride from *Kill Bill*, and a UT student with a cleaver in his head. A pirate and Little Orphan Annie made out languidly on a corner.

Ten Great Eating Streets in the United States

1. South Congress Avenue—Austin
2. Nicollet Avenue—Minneapolis, Minnesota
3. Milwaukee Street—Milwaukee, Wisconsin (duh)
4. St. Clair Avenue—Cleveland, Ohio
5. Smith Street—Brooklyn, New York
6. The Embarcadero—San Francisco, California
7. Cambridge Avenue—Boston, Massachusetts
8. Highland Avenue—Atlanta, Georgia
9. Broadway north of West 72nd Street—New York, New York
10. Northwest 23rd Avenue—Portland, Oregon

Al pastor pork is prepared like Middle Eastern sha-warma, the dish from which it is actually descended. The pork is marinated for one to two days, then slow-roasted and carved off of a rotating spit.

We headed toward our hotel, dodging costumed and drunken students. I passed three bleeding demons clad in black and Ricky Bobby, all already deep in their cups and having a hard time with gravity and inertia.

After a short break at the hotel, during which I saw some of a Yankee game (which they ended up winning), I put on my costume and headed to a taco truck on South Congress (SoCo to the natives) I'd heard about where the three-al-pastor-tacos-for-five-bucks plate was "the bomb-ass deal."

I rolled up to the truck with Danielle in tow, and we took a place in line behind a bearded dude dressed as Dorothy, the Travelocity Roaming Gnome, and a big bunny rabbit. I ordered my tacos and waited behind a large dude in a Hawaiian shirt and perhaps the cheesiest man ever in a tuxedo, who struck a *GQ* pose whenever a woman walked by. We ate our tacos as we walked. They had tender, spicy, and almost buttery meat with homemade salsas roja and verde. We enjoyed their deliciousness while heading downtown, downing our last bites before joining the crowds in the blocks that were closed off for foot traffic and debauchery.

The scene when we arrived was already utter madness. Everyone drunk or drinking, everyone laughing, music emanating from every bar and alleyway, Princess Leia deep-tonguing Luke on a police barrier. I witnessed Sodom and Gomorrah–like behavior that was unlike anything I had ever seen. We joined the celebration for a time, and with way more restraint than many of our fellow revelers. I was excited and into it for a bit, then got scared like a little bitch and ran back to my hotel.

Oh, and my costume?

Kim Jong-illin'.

It made sense at the time.

The next afternoon, we headed back down to SoCo to return Danielle's costume at Lucy in Disguise with Diamonds. After waiting with every hungover UT grad in the city on a line that rivaled the DMV's in length, we went for some chow. South Congress has a collection of legendary food stands—actually, trailers, to be more accurate. Some are strictly dessert-based like Hey Cupcake! which sells, well, cupcakes, and Austin Gourmet Pudding, which is a super-tiny shack that peddles pudding. Others have the savory stuff, like the one we hit up: the amazing Mighty Cone.

I had seen this place on past visits to Austin, but never tried it. I was a fool. A damn fool. Mighty Cone is the brainchild of restaurateurs who own a fine-dining establishment elsewhere in Austin, and their Hot and Crunchy cones—so-called because they're served in paper drink cones—are things of sheer wonder. The secret is the coating—a mix of sesame seeds, arbol chile flakes, ground almonds, sea salt, sugar, and corn flakes—they use to batter shrimp and/or chicken that is then fried and served with or without avocado. The avocado—and you know how I feel about avocados—is also coated and fried or, as they say, deep sautéed, and available as its own cone. It all goes into a tortilla to be topped with a mango-jalapeño slaw and ancho sauce that I can only describe as pure awesomeness.

The result is a pregnant woman's dream, a combination of sweet, salty, and crunchy. And need I explain the sheer sexiness of a deep-fried avocado?

I didn't think so.

We each gobbled down a cone, then tried their sliders, which came with fries and yet another phenomenal condiment: roasted red pepper ketchup. Mighty Cone, you have ruined me like an innocent on prom night. French fries will never be the same.

A SLIDER FROM MIGHTY CONE

I had fully intended to leave Austin that night, but I needed just one more day. Or, more accurately, one more night. Maybe it was the siren song of the city.

After all, one cannot go to Austin without catching some live music, and on that occasion it turned out that one of my favorite live acts, Gogol Bordello, was playing the renowned venue Stubb's BBQ. Lacking a hotel reservation, it took me a bit to find another place to stay, by which time the show had begun (and Danielle had decided that she'd had her fill of going out). I headed to the club just in case there was enough show left to try to see. They'd finished playing, but a cool dude who recognized me from TV pulled me aside and told me that Gogol Bordello was going to play a secret after-hours show later that night at a spot called Lovejoys. Sweet! Plus time to eat beforehand. I headed to Casino el Camino, which a local had told me has the best burgers in town.

It turned out to be a dark, somewhat cavernous bar on East Sixth (aka Old Pecan Street) known for stiff drinks, good music, and great food—in particular verde chili fries and burgers. I did a few shots of Dripping Springs, a local vodka, then walked to the kitchen window at the back of the restaurant. The very cool kitchen manager James "Puppy" Evertt (yes, "Puppy"; what part of "Keep Austin Weird" didn't you get?) explained that you can't eat in Austin, much less at Casino el Camino, without having roasted chiles and salsa verde. Under his approving eye I ordered the Amarillo Burger, which comes with roasted serrano chiles, jalapeño jack cheese, and cilantro mayonnaise (all Southwest flavor staples), along with some of their famous verde chili fries (fries with tomatillo salsa verde and melted cheese).

A drink later, my name was called and I went back to the kitchen to pick up my food. I have to say that I loved the fact that you have to get off your ass to order and pick up your own food straight from the kitchen. As I walked back to the bar with my laden tray, Puppy called out, "Be strange, but don't be a stranger!" the best farewell I've heard in all my years, and perfect for Austin.

My burger was soft and perfectly medium rare, and each bite was deliciously, deliriously spicy from the chiles and jalapeño cheese until the cilantro mayo came in and chilled everybody out. Sublime. The verde chile fries were crispy, somewhat salty, and most importantly skin-on. The cheese somehow never hardened and the tomatillo salsa was freshly made. In fact, Puppy had made it a point to tell me that he had just made it. And the man did not lie. Just stupendous, and a perfect coda to my Austin adventure.

Lovejoys, a relatively unassuming club on Neches Street, turned out to be less than a block from Casino el Camino, and I walked right in. And I must say I had on a shit-eating grin from the moment I darkened the doorway till I left (and not just because there was no bullshit cover charge). There was Eugene Hutz, the Gogol Bordello front man, on the tiny stage that rose barely eight inches above the club floor, surrounded by accordion players, trumpet players, and a whirling, twirling swarm of Austinites dancing in gypsylike ecstasy around him. No bouncers, no boundaries. No place else on earth could this happen. I grabbed a shot of whiskey, a bottle of Lone Star, and the hand of a pretty girl and danced and swirled amongst the weird and the wonderful in a haze of smoke and balalaika strains. I stood on a chair and laughed, and took pictures, and locked arms and swung strangers about. I rejoiced over my night, my finds, my friends, my beautiful Austin that welcomed me into her delicious, weird bosom, nursed me with chiles and goose bumps, kissed me with vodka and verde, and rocked me to sleep with a blissful Balkan lullaby. Trick or treat? Austin—like the best of us—is both.

BLUEBERRY MUSTARD
from Moonshine Patio Bar and Grill in Austin

This recipe is adapted from the one used at the Moonshine Patio Bar and Grill. It's pretty much the best condiment ever. They serve it with their corn dog, but it can go with just about anything that you would add mustard to. See my suggestion for having it with grilled lobster (page 210).

2 cups blueberries, fresh or frozen and defrosted

1 teaspoon fresh lemon juice

1 tablespoon sugar

1½ cups yellow mustard

1½ cups mayonnaise

½ cup honey

½ cup Dijon mustard

2 tablespoons apple cider vinegar

½ teaspoon cayenne

1 teaspoon salt

1 teaspoon ground black pepper

2 tablespoons fresh tarragon leaves, finely chopped

Combine the blueberries, lemon juice, sugar, and 2 tablespoons water in a blender and blend until smooth. Measure out ½ cup, and reserve or freeze the rest for another use. In a bowl, stir together the ½ cup blueberry puree and 1 cup of the yellow mustard.

In a separate bowl, combine the mayonnaise, honey, Dijon mustard, vinegar, cayenne, salt, papper, and tarragon leaves. Mix until thoroughly blended.

Cover both bowls and refrigerate until ready to serve.

To serve, scoop about ¼ cup of the honey-mustard mixture into a small bowl. Swirl in about 1 tablespoon of the blueberry puree, but don't combine them completely.

(You can store the two mixtures for up to a week in the refrigerator, but keep them in separate bowls and don't mix them until you're ready to serve.)

✦ ✦ ✦

CHAPTER 7

DID THE EARTH MOVE?

A Brush with Unrequited Love and Other Natural Disasters

✦ ✦ ✦

SAN FRANCISCO, CA

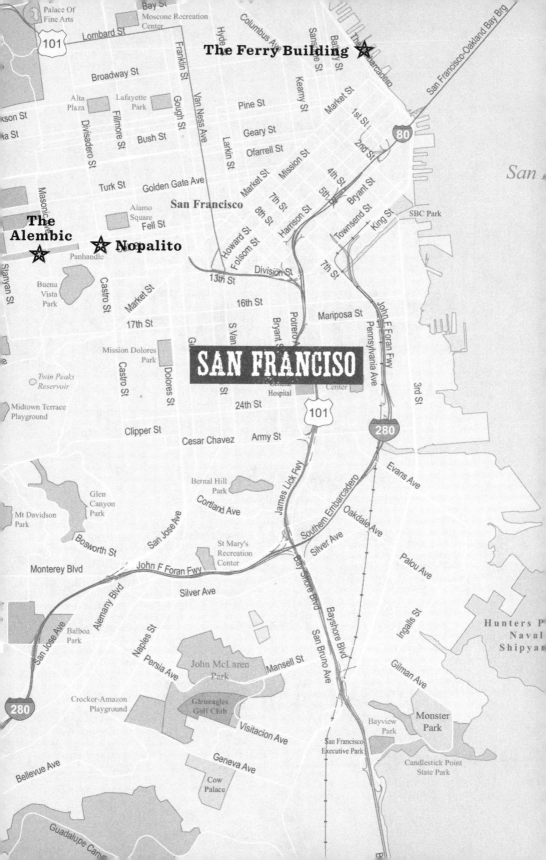

Market Street.

I'd walked its length with a teen tour at age 14.

Shopped in its stores with my grandma when I was living and working in San Jose, a few hours south.

Watched a knife fight near its intersection with Fifth from the window of a hotel in the Tenderloin that fancied itself more of a gentrifying force in the area than it actually was.

And now here I was again.

Walking up Market alone, I was mesmerized by the wide thoroughfare, the beautiful architecture that lined it, and the cat's cradle of interwoven trolley cables above and intrigued by the smaller streets that slashed across it diagonally to lead one to Chinatown, Union Square, SoMa (South of Market), and even the delightfully undelightful Tenderloin.

San Francisco is a city that lends itself to romance, with impossibly cool neighborhoods lined with beautiful Victorian homes, views of the water on three sides, and countless little side streets to explore, get lost in, have adventures on. It's hard to remain unmoved by the mystery and sexiness of feeling the fog roll over you, the inherent sultriness of uttering the word "Embarcadero," or the fact that America's great wine country is mere miles to the north. It's a city dotted with steep hills, coursed by vintage trolleys, steeped in the wanderlust of generations past. And, "high on a hill," it called to my heart, just as it did to Tony Bennett's in his iconic tribute to the town. It was ripe with potential if not my own happy experience.

Now, there are *gorgeous* women in San Francisco—like, Helen of Troy gorgeous—so the obstacle had not been a lack of those to woo. It had been a combination of shitty luck, worse timing, and the unfortunate realizations that not one, but two relationships just didn't have the juice to go the distance. Both of these revelations had come while eating delicious seafood at Fisherman's Wharf.

I was back on Market Street.

And I was alone.

I headed toward the water, past the Tenderloin, past the zig-zagging streets I'd traversed just a few years earlier arm in arm with a glorious, deeply intelligent green-eyed girl who shared a sumptuous dim sum feast with me in Chinatown before telling me she didn't kiss on the first date.

I walked on up Market Street till there was no more Market Street. Past booths of artisans selling everything from necklaces to flattened wine bottles to be used as spoon rests.

I walked across the trolley tracks toward the Embarcadero and the water and finally arrived at a massive, pale blue–gray structure

topped by a massive clock tower: the Ferry Building. entered to find a skylit maze of shops, all aglow with the local, fresh, sea-sonal best of the Bay Area. Stores selling nothing but mushrooms, or olive oil, or beef and beef jerky. There were sit-down eat-eries and lunch counters, gro-ceries and granaries. It was all the bounty of the Bay under one roof, and I was ready to drown my malaise in delish.

I stopped at Boccalone,

chef Chris Cosentino's (of Food Net-
work fame) outpost for "tasty salted
pig parts," a clean, light, airy shop
with red lockers for hanging and
cooling salami and such. I wasn't
sure where to begin—I mean, they
had *spreadable salame*!!! I ended
up getting a little charcuterie sample cone with coppa di testa (like
headcheese, with pig bits pressed
together), capicola, and salame
pepato. I was struck by the creaminess of all the meats, and though

they'd all been cured, there was no overwhelming saltiness. They
suggested I try their lardo—essentially, cured fat—which
I thought would be a little too much until they put it on some awesome crusty bread with local preserves and it became something
out of this flippin' world. I ended up buying a brown sugar and
fennel salame.

But what's cured meat without cheese? On the staff's recommendation, I headed virtually next door to local cheesemonger Cowgirl Creamery. Their equally well-informed, white-aproned staff
walked me through a whole bunch of local cheeses from Sonoma,
Petaluma, and Point Reyes that ran the gamut from runny, funky,
washed-rind triple-crème cheeses to harder, firmer specimens. Their
own cheeses were simply incredible, the Crocodile Tear and Red
Hawk especially, and I was even more blown away by the fact that I
was tasting salami and cheeses made within a stone's throw of Silicon Valley. I bought a few hunks to take home with me: the brie-like
Red Hawk, some crumbly and nutty dry jack, and Humboldt Fog, a
creamy cheese bisected with a layer of pine ash.

THE CROCODILE TEAR CHEESE AT COWGIRL CREAMERY

Salame? Check. Cheese? Check.

All I needed was the bread, and at the suggestion of the pretty cheesemonger who helped me at Cowgirl, I headed off to Acme Bread Company—next door.

The place looks like a children's book illustration of a bread market, with wooden bins holding baskets of rustic country loaves, a marble countertop with even more leavened artistry piled upon it, and white-aproned bakers pushing baking racks in the back. The loaf that had gotten my cheesemonger's nod was the *pain d'epi* made with organic wheat flour and barley flour and shaped like an olive branch, with crusty bits flanging off each side of the loaf. However, the lady behind Acme's counter said she considered the pain au levain, a crusty, round, specially leavened rustic loaf that would not have been out of place in the French countryside, their crown jewel. I asked her if she felt that the abundance of decadently crusty bread—sourdough and otherwise—in San Fran was a direct result of the city's high ambient moisture and humidity, and she agreed that it absolutely was. In fact, she explained, the breads made using the same recipes at the bakery's other outpost in Berkeley were completely different from these, made and sold mere feet from the water.

I had local salame, local cheese, local bread, and now I needed a local beverage—something with enough acidity to cut through the richness of the meat and cheese. It was a little too early for wine, so I headed to another Bay Area stalwart, also conveniently located in the very same building, Blue Bottle Coffee.

The length of the line that greeted me was just stupid. Truly. But I'd heard such great things, I figured it must obviously be worth the wait and dutifully took my place at the end of the endless queue. Now, waiting on line for food and beverages is never my favorite thing, but on this occasion I was unlucky enough to have a particularly effete middle-aged gentleman behind me, and he was a total douche. When I stepped a foot out of line to look at the bags of freshly roasted, hand-stamped beans, he quickly jumped ahead and glared at me through what must have been inch-thick glasses when I attempted to return to my place. After realizing that I would more than likely stomp a mudhole in his ass if he didn't let me back in, he eventually yielded and allowed me back in line. And then I realized that what I'd picked up was decaf (*yuck*). I stepped out to change beans, keeping one foot firmly planted on line, only to have this guy jump ahead again. I stepped up to him and glared. He froze.

"Really?" I said.

He stood there, unmoving. Defiant? Deaf? Afraid?

"Can I help you?" asked the barista, who was probably 20 years old and looked 14. The situation somewhat diffused, I ordered a coffee and paid for my beans. As I turned to leave, I asked a simple question, something along the lines of "Where are the lids?" and the eye-rolling exasperation that emanated from this prepubescent toadstool was as thick as the headgear of the asshole behind me.

"That's it, Blue Bottle!" I thought. "I don't care how good your coffee is, you attract idiots and employ supercilious snobs!" Too much time on my own had left me as bitter as dark-roasted arabica, I guess. I hoped it would be worth the ordeal.

And oh my, was it ever, more syrupy than most coffee, with a finish tasting of caramel and chicory.

I headed outside to grab a bench by the water.

Young, impossibly well-coiffed San Fran intelligentsia and

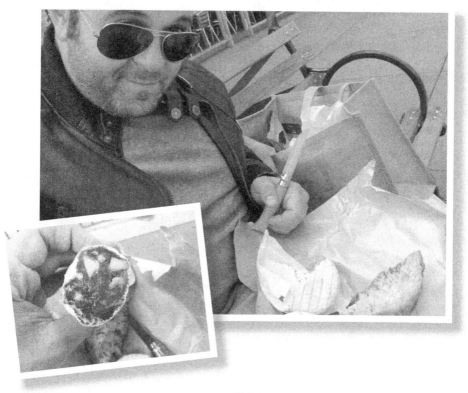

yuppies occupied nearly every bench, fiddling with a vast array of modern gadgets: iPhones, iPads, iThises, iThats. A boat labeled "Mendocino" drifted idly toward the Bay Bridge as I prepared to dive into my moveable feast.

The crusty, hoppy bread was the ideal canvas on which to paint the buttery, redolent cheeses and the sweet, salty salame. Swigs of the dark coffee cut through the lot and rounded out the perfect, chilly summer San Fran afternoon.

Thus fortified, I walked along the Embarcadero to Fisherman's Wharf, where loud, olive-skinned men harangued tourists to enter their restaurants for chowder and crabmeat-stuffed avocados. I did a one-eighty and headed back up the Embarcadero toward my hotel, feeling more optimistic about the night ahead of me, as the sun began to slip behind the City on the Bay.

San Francisco, one the nation's largest and most densely populated cities, is a rare wonder. For some it has been a haven for countercultural expression, including the hippie, free-love contingent that called the city's Haight-Ashbury district home; the Beat poets (and the modern-day hipsters who strive to channel them) who embraced the North Beach area; and the gay community that created a supportive stronghold in the Castro. The City by the Bay wears its history like a badge of honor, yet it thrives on innovation in harmony with antiquity. Modern skyscrapers like the Transamerica Pyramid dwell companionably beside the art deco Coit Tower and a watercolor palette of hillside Victorian homes, Beaux Arts structures like City Hall and the Palace of Fine Arts, and some of the most incredible Asia-influenced designs in the United States.

161

It also bears noting that in terms of landmarks, this city possesses as many iconic locations as New York, if not more, and far more than any other place in California. Without even trying you can probably name a dozen: Fisherman's Wharf, the Embarcadero, the Golden Gate and Bay bridges, Alcatraz, Chinatown, Coit Tower, the Presidio, Lombard Street, Ghirardelli Square, and on and on.

These monuments are essential to the economy. With much of the city's shipping business having moved across the bay to Oakland, San Francisco relies heavily on its tourism industry as a source of revenue.

Many of those icons represent an age gone by, when the city formerly known as Yerba Buena grew as a shipping hub because of its proximity to water and its solvency, and also because of its geological kick-assery. Yup, I'm talkin' silver and gold. Between the Gold Rush of 1849 (from which the 49ers football team takes its name) and the discovery of the Comstock Lode 10 years later, San Fran's population nearly doubled, and it continued to grow rapidly over the next 10 years; in 1870, it was more than four times what it had been in 1850. This boom brought prosperity (and some lawlessness for a bit), culture, wave upon wave of immigration, and booming trade to the newly launched Port of San Francisco. With an ever-expanding variety of cultures and industries flourishing in the city, new businesses and neighborhoods popped up to satisfy the tastes of these diverse communities.

True Fact: When the stock market crashed in 1929, San Francisco was so financially solid that not one of its banks went under.

Among the most successful of these new residents was Italian immigrant Domingo Ghirardelli, who came to San Fran in 1849 with dreams of finding gold. After failing at mining, he sold supplies and confections to miners from a tent in Stockton; he later opened a San Fran store and hotel, which burned down in 1851. Determined as ever, in 1852 he formed the confectionary company that today is called the Ghirardelli Chocolate Company, and it remains hugely successful more than 150 years later.

At this same time, former Chinese railroad workers and miners created San Francisco's Chinatown quarter, and the regional Cantonese, Hunan, and Szechuan cuisines served in the early restaurants helped to shape the Chinese American cuisine that we know today. It is the oldest Chinatown in North America, and home to the largest Chinese community outside of Asia.

It's also important to acknowledge San Fran's Latin roots. Though less pronounced than in Los Angeles to the south, the Latin influence on the city and its menus is pervasive.

More recently, the dot-com boom brought an influx of wealthy, young, white-collar professionals to the Bay Area looking for a taste of that sweet Silicon success. As a result, since the late 1990s, many previously unsavory neighborhoods have been gentrified and the city has established itself at the vanguard of progressive urban culture.

But it wasn't just the moolah and boutiques that came with

In 2008, more than 30% of San Francisco's population was Asian, compared to just over 54% non-Hispanic whites.

Some Other Great Markets to Check Out

1. Shaker Square Farmers Market—Cleveland, Ohio
2. Union Square Greenmarket—New York, New York
3. Montgomery Curb Market—Montgomery, Alabama
4. West Side Market—Cleveland, Ohio
5. Eastern Market—Washington, DC
6. Reading Terminal Market—Philadelphia, Pennsylvania
7. Farmers Market Annex—Minneapolis, Minnesota
8. Dane County Farmers' Market—Madison, Wisconsin

these people, it was also their tastes and, more importantly, their taste buds. While previous generations had focused on the foods of their respective homelands, the culinary sensibilities of the "new" San Francisco intelligentsia spurred a citywide organic, seasonal, free-range, locavore–based food movement. This has resulted in some really great, wholesome artisanal food.

But what I find so dope about San Fran is that the inherent artistry of the gourmet small-batch breads, coffees, cheeses, and meats one finds here transcends the typical health- and weight-conscious California fare, synthesizing play and passion, comfort food and haute cuisine. Armed with the best of nearly every type of produce, most of which is grown directly to the south or north of the city, and a fishing industry that teems with exquisite local products like Dungeness crab, sand dabs, and bay shrimp, the chefs of San Francisco have a leg up on their competition in every other city, and they often far surpass them. There seems to be a widespread determination to produce the very best food possible—and from what I've tasted, they often succeed in this goal.

While Los Angeles is the shimmery tinsel star of Southern California, San Fran is in NorCal, and it's a different animal altogether. And geography is only one of the natural factors that influence San Francisco's dining tables.

Unlike other parts of sunny California, San Francisco can be rather wet. It is, after all, located on a peninsula, surrounded by water on three sides. The climate, like much of the rest of California's coastline, can be categorized as Mediterranean, with wet winters and dry summers. The hills that San Fran is famous for create microclimates, which spawn little weather systems that bring about weird occurrences like fog in the summer and huge variances in rainfall from one part of the city to the next.

Geologically speaking, San Francisco sits just north of the San Andreas fault, which, like most fault lines, has brought some of the land's rich geologic treasures (gold, silver, vital minerals) to the surface—and also makes the area vulnerable to the earthquakes that all but leveled it in 1906 and caused hellacious damage in 1989.

Today, the several-times-rebuilt City by the Bay thrives on the biodiversity made possible by its location. It is still a major shipping point, making goods from the world over readily available to the fertile culinary minds that are all too eager to devour these amazing foodstuffs from varied ports of call and to embrace the city's ethnic diversity and integrate it into the foods made for the second- and third-generation descendants of the people who helped build this haven on the bay.

Couple *that* with the fact that the palate of the average modern San Franciscan is quite sophisticated, and you get culturally diverse cuisine that is a perfect hybrid of tradition and innovation, past and present—much like the architecture of the city.

☆　☆　☆

Which brings me back to Market Street.

Alone.

But not for long.

A good friend of mine had set me up on a date with a friend, and anticipation coursed through me like the jump-juice pushing the trolley cars beside me. I headed to my hotel, spruced up, attempted to find my inner Tony Bennett, and went downstairs to meet my date, an angel with anime-big almond eyes deeper, warmer, sweeter, and more honeyed brown than anything Domingo Ghirardelli ever concocted in his sweet shop.

Our tentative first stabs at conversation were not nearly as awkward as I had feared they would be, and we laughed as the ice was broken, thawed, and melted into the foggy bay. My eyes lingered on the rose tattoo on her shoulder. Again, and again, and again.

THE ALEMBIC

Great People to Get Authentic Local Restaurant
Recommendations From

1. Bellhops
2. Parking attendants (especially at municipal garages)
3. Waitstaff at a restaurant you like (but only if the
   place is privately owned and not a chain; otherwise,
   they may just send you to another property they have
   a stake in)
4. Butchers and fishmongers
5. Fruit and vegetable purveyors at local farmers'
   markets (they may even send you to a place they
   supply with fresh produce!)

We headed to The Alembic, a gastropub on Haight that a local friend had recommended. Now, to a New Yorker like me, gastropubs—by definition watering holes with an elevated spirits selection and even more elevated epicurean bar bites—are hardly news, and sadly they have become the province of food-snob douche bags who feel validated and "downtowny" by eating sweetbreads and swilling craft beer. (I say this having eaten and swilled both—kettle, meet pot.) But I trusted my friend because she is a) a local, b) not a douche, and c) a woman, and experience has taught me that they are in fact smarter than we hairy-chested mouthbreathers.

The place would not have been out of place back home in Brooklyn; its long, narrow footprint, stamped-metal ceilings, and low lighting called to mind the artisanal eateries of Smith Street, Brooklyn's Restaurant Row. As we walked in, we saw at the bar to our left a huge blackboard listing the special tipples of the house and, above us, rack after rack of bottles that loomed as high as the ceiling.

We grabbed a seat in the back, not too far from the kitchen, where food specials were listed on yet another blackboard.

Led Zeppelin provided that night's soundtrack, which I took to be a good omen, as I worship at the altar of Zep's unrelenting awesomeness. My date had heard *of* them, but had not *heard* them, making me feel both old *and* obligated to educate her in the ways of Zeppelin. She listened and laughed as I passionately described the Viking imagery in "Immigrant Song" and pointed out the Beastie Boys' sampling of "When the Levee Breaks." We talked and flirted for a while and then, after a bit, looked at the massive spirits list, ultimately deciding on a few of their signature cocktails.

I chose something called the Vice Grip, the perfect cocktail for an indecisive diner like myself, as it contained Araku Rum and Coffee Liqueur; a sweet, faintly berrylike, slightly sparkling, low-alcohol red wine from Northwestern Italy called Brachetto d'Acqui; and porter foam. As the menu says, "That's liquor, wine, coffee, and beer all in the same glass. What you do with the rest of your night is up to you." Yup. In keeping with the prevailing trend toward "mixology" rather than straight bartending, the drinks were relatively small, pretty, and packed a capital *W* wallop, veritable symphonies of spirits, sprigs, splashes, and dashes. Mine had a thick head of foam and a color that hovered between plum, porter, and Robitussin.

I looked across the table at the girl with the rose tattoo, who raised her drink (served in a shallow glass allegedly cast in the shape of Marie Antoinette's breast).

"What should we drink to?"

"Umm . . . lady's choice."

"Cop out."

"No, no. I'll take the next one."

"Deal." She thought for a moment, curling her perfect pink lips over her teeth, and cast her amber eyes at the ceiling like a little girl at a spelling bee. "To embracing the moment," she announced.

"To embracing the moment."

Clink.

The flavor was intense, a straight bitch slap to my mouth. The coffee rose like smoke from the back of my tongue to my soft palate, the sweet acidity of the wine curled the sides of my tongue and made my gums shudder, the fizz from the porter popped off the backs of my teeth and lips, and the liquor stomped down the middle of my tongue like Boss Tweed.

Hell yeah, Vice Grip. Hell yeah. What I did with the rest of my night *was* up to me . . .

"How is your drink?" I asked her.

"Awesome. It's pretty unbelievable actually. I like whiskey and . . . "

"Wait, you like whiskey?"

"Yeah. And they've kind of made whiskey sophisticated, but still let it be whiskey. That's really amazing."

"What's it called again?"

"Vow of Silence. The name was half the reason I ordered it. I like this place."

"Me, too."

"Might like you, too."

"Might?"

"Yup."

Pub covered. On to the gastro.

"Let's order."

And dear Lord did we order. We ordered with the force of a thousand suns. Luckily, there was an empty table beside us to accommodate our overflow, a sort of "feeder" table if you will. Now bear in mind that at many gastropubs, this one included, the plates, much like the drinks, are on the small side but pack a punch, so one can order a variety of dishes without being overwhelmed by the amount of food. That said, I was so dazzled by the amazing array of seasonal *and* local ingredients the menu promised that I wanted to try damn near everything—and nearly did. Just recalling the tastes of what we ordered sets me aglow with delight): duck hearts with pickled pineapple; wagyu beef tongue sliders with fried green tomatoes, horseradish, and pickled red onion; local shishito peppers with house-smoked salt; bone marrow with garlic confit; and crispy pork belly and scallops with English peas, corn puree, and trumpet mushrooms, all boasting local ingredients. Even the salt was local. Oh wait! There's also local cheese? Sure, we'll try that, too! We went with Bellwether carmody and camellia—two cheeses from nearby Petaluma and Sonoma.

I could write a veritable *War and Peace* extolling the excellence of each dish and not exaggerate one iota, but in the interest of time and preserving your patience, I will give you the *SportsCenter* highlight package.

The duck hearts were fucking incredible. Now, for all of you who freak out about offal, don't trip—there was no gaminess to this dish *at all*. Truth be told, it tasted like a great cut of filet, with a sear and charred flavor reminiscent of Korean barbecue. The pickled pineapple brought a contrast not unlike chutney or Indian mango pickle.

WAGYU BEEF TONGUE SLIDERS

The sliders were just plain great, the tongue butter-tender, and the fried green tomatoes—always a risky addition to a sandwich as they can soggy up most any bread if done poorly—crisp and light with that perfect tart sourness.

"I'll just take a bite of the slider," my date said. "You can finish mine. I won't want the whole thing."

Bite.

"No, no, I was wrong. I'm gonna eat the whole thing and yours too if you don't get to it first."

And then the marrow. Oh, the marrow, the denatured protein so often overlooked and miscategorized as fat. The rich, unctuous, buttery essence of roasted meat, in this case covered with soft, pungent, and sweet garlic confit and capers. I loved that this place, rather than cut across the bone to make disks or cylinders, cut the bone *lengthwise* to let more of the marrow develop a beautiful crust from the roasting and to make the scooping of it all the easier. I spread some on the great crusty bread that was served alongside it and passed it to my date, who'd never tried it before. She took a bite and chewed thoughtfully before saying:

MARROW, SWEET MARROW

"So basically it's like the absolute best butter ever."

"Pretty damn close, yeah." It was incredible. Smoky, salty, meaty, silky in many ways, and cut perfectly by the acidity of the capers and the sweet stink of the garlic.

The shishito peppers emerged as my date's favorite, smoky,

salty, and with a great flavor somewhere between green bell pepper and heaven.

And let's not forget the union that all foodies can get behind, scallops and pork belly. Or should I say "holy" and "shit"? The dish looked gorgeous, but I hadn't come just to look. The scallops were immaculately fresh and felt to the mouth and to the fork like flan, custard, or foie gras, with no graininess or toughness whatsoever. And the pork belly was like decadent meat caramel that liquified on the tongue almost instantly, giving way to the cracker-crunch of the seared meat. But the true revelation of this dish was its underpinning, the most delicious and memorable use of peas I've ever encountered. Usually I eat them because they're there, but there's usually "no there there" (to quote Gertrude Stein). These peas, however, were firm, sweet, grassy, and perfect.

We ate, we laughed, we ended up holding hands.

The kitchen was out of coffee by the time we were done with our meal, the only chink in the otherwise stupendous performance. But we were in the Haight and feeling radical, so we just stayed with the cocktail menu. Throwing caution to the wind and breaking a cardinal drinking maxim, I mixed liquors, choosing for my second drink another towering triumph called the Southern Exposure. Gin, lime juice, mint, and celery juice. Refreshing and, believe it or not, actually a great palate cleanser.

After a seriously artsy-fartsy, badass dessert of olive oil cake served with a chocolate ganache/pudding/budino, passion fruit mousse, and sea salt and another, a special of pink-peppercorn-flecked shingles of meringue set artistically askew over a perfectly rectangular bar of pale yellow yuzu curd and ruby-red poached strawberries that looked like an exhibit in the Whitney Biennial, we sat there, fingers of both hands interlocked across the small wooden table, her eyes reflecting yellow candlelight back at me. Dinner had gone better than either of us could have hoped.

"Let's get a cab," she said.

"Let's."

We stood up from the table.

"Hey wait," she said, gesturing to the last few swigs of our drinks, "you never did the second toast!"

"You're right, I didn't."

"Go on. Do it now."

"For real?"

"Uh-huh."

And I thought of the evening we'd shared. Little, powerful drinks. Dishes with equal parts head, heart, and *hearth*. Local, lovable, and clever as hell. Delicious, decadent, and I got to share it with this woman standing across from me. This beauty with her hip cocked, her *Flashdance*-necked white T-shirt slipping off her shoulder, and that damned rose tattoo. She ate with me, she drank with me, she held my hand—no, make that *hands*—and she just might like me. This girl with the flickering amber eyes just might like me. She was raising her glass, looking at me, and wanting to know what we were celebrating tonight.

"To San Francisco."

I'd like to say we made love and laughed and giggled till dawn.

But I'd be lying.

The next day found me as ever—alone on Market Street.

Happier somewhat, but no less alone.

Phone rang and it was the girl from the dim sum date eons ago. Somehow she knew I was in town and she wanted to have dinner. I figured, hey, it's the second date now, right?

We met and she looked better than ever, a firecracker with emerald eyes and a sharp tongue. We headed over to Nopalito, a restaurant in Lower Haight not far off Divisadero. A place that described itself as "a vibrant neighborhood Mexican kitchen celebrating the traditional cookery of Mexico and utilizing our philosophy of purchasing local, organic, and sustainable ingredients." Mexico by way of San Fran—I'm in.

We ordered an incredible ceviche with rock cod, squid, tomatillo, avocado, and cilantro, all of which tasted incredibly fresh; a salad of mixed varieties of cucumber; and quite possibly one of the greatest quesadillas in Christendom, stuffed with squash blossoms, leeks, zucchini, salsa negra, and queso fresco. The veggies were so fresh, even the corn tortilla tasted more corn than tortilla.

And the place just kept kicking ass right through the entrées. We actually had a small war of attrition going on across the table until I finally agreed to surrender the pitch-perfect pescado a la talla, lingcod seared with ancho and guajillo chiles, as I tucked into her order of Nopalito's renowned carnitas, deeply tender *slooooooooowwwwww*-braised pork with hints of orange and bay leaf served with a mind-blowingly fresh tomatillo salsa and  beer cabbage salad. I used the fresh tortillas to make mini tacos with the pork and can say that it was without question the lightest

Mexican meal I've ever eaten, yet completely satisfying and substantial. The fact that their margaritas and cocktails rocked (especially the El Diablo and Ponche Nopalito) didn't hurt either.

As we walked up the street after our meal, much to my surprise, she took my arm and rested her head on my shoulder. I felt 10 feet tall.

"So, this would be our *second* date, right?" I asked hopefully.

"Ummm. Yeah, I guess so."

"Does that mean I can smooch you?"

"No."

"Ah."

"It's not that. I just got out of a thing and . . . "

"You're not ready for a new thing. I get it."

"It's just bad timing."

"It's just me and San Fran."

"No, it's just bad timing. You're always going on about how you love this city—it's not SF."

"No? Then how come every time I come close to coming close to someone here, it slips away?"

"It's bad timing, wrong people, who knows—but don't blame the city. Haven't you had a nice time here?"

"I have."

"Don't you like spending time with me?"

"Of course I do."

"So . . . ?"

"So, as amazing as this place is, it fills me with warmth and wonder and I want someone to share it with and I've never once had that."

"We're sharing it, aren't we?" she said while looking up at me with those green lasers.

"We are," I conceded, "we are." I stopped walking, put my hands on her tiny waist. Ran the backs of my fingers across her tan cheek, tucked a wavy tendril of hair behind her soft ear. She smiled at me and crinkled up her nose. I touched her lips with my thumb and brought her face toward mine.

"I can't," she said.

I let go of her, dropped my arms to my sides and my chin to my chest.

Fine.

I give over.

I shall love the city streets, the small-batch craft chocolates and beers and Vietnamese sandwiches and cable cars and pastel clapboard houses that rise on scattered hillsides like in Verona. I shall enjoy the breeze, the low-lying fog, the culture, the commerce, the style, substance, and superior Szechuan—and I will do it alone. I will no longer try. I will . . .

"I want a third date, Adam," she said as she raised my chin with a slender finger. "Come back. Come back soon."

"I will."

Maybe I left a piece of it there after all.

NOPALITO'S SALSA VERDE

Makes about 2 cups

The restaurant refers to this as *salsa cruda*, or raw salsa, as all the ingredients are combined raw, giving it a bright green color and flavor.

4 organic jalapeños, ribs and seeds removed, cut into ¼-inch pieces

14 organic tomatillos, husked and cut into ¼-inch pieces

3 organic garlic cloves, peeled and coarsely chopped

½ bunch organic cilantro, leaves and stems, chopped

Salt to taste

Combine all the salsa ingredients in a blender or food processor and blend on medium-high speed until nearly pureed. The mixture should be smooth, but with a bit of texture.

This salsa is best used the day it is made but will keep, tightly covered in the refrigerator, for up to 4 days.

CHAPTER 8

☆ ☆ ☆

THE LOBSTER ROLL: WHY I WANT TO HAVE SEX WITH ONE

Or: A Good Roll Is Hard to Find

☆ ☆ ☆

PORTLAND, ME

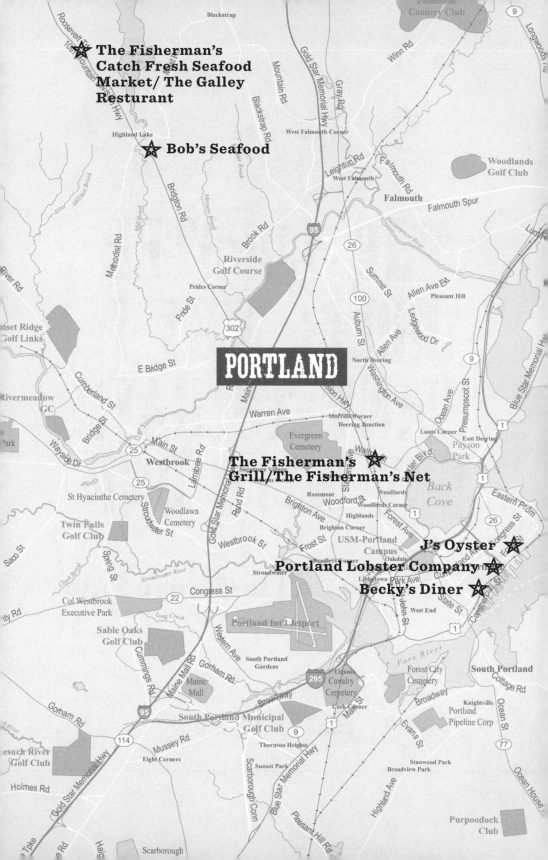

The Fisherman's Catch Fresh Seafood Market/ The Galley Resturant

Bob's Seafood

Highland Lake

PORTLAND

The Fisherman's Grill/The Fisherman's Net

J's Oyster

Portland Lobster Company

Becky's Diner

I am a city mouse.

I am.

I've hiked, I've camped, I've kayaked, canoed, and trekked.

I have communed or made efforts to that effect with the natural world around me.

I have slept in dirt, been bitten by spiders, and slept in a pyramid of waxed canvas in national parks.

I have enjoyed these experiences.

To an extent.

While I love being around natural beauty, immersing myself in it, interacting with it, and so on, I would not opt to live in it.

I admit it.

I like air-conditioning, the peace of mind of a locked door, walls, ceilings, floors, and modern plumbing.

Now, while I was certainly not roughing it, circumstances and a wedding had placed me about 40 minutes north of Portland in the town of South Casco, on the banks of beautiful Sebago Lake—the biggest lake in the southwestern corner of Maine and indisputably a huge vacation mecca. This area of Maine is all pine trees and lakes, marinas and vacation beaches. Cars towing boats and motor homes. And while I love my friend, had a blast at his beautiful wedding, and wish he and his new bride unending happiness, my time in the wilds of South Casco was marred by my stay in a cramped, bug-ridden cabin with shitty light, worse ventilation, and an unlockable door. Add to my accommodations at the House of Usher my date getting sick, and mosquitoes big enough to carry off a toddler biting my left hand so badly that not only did I look

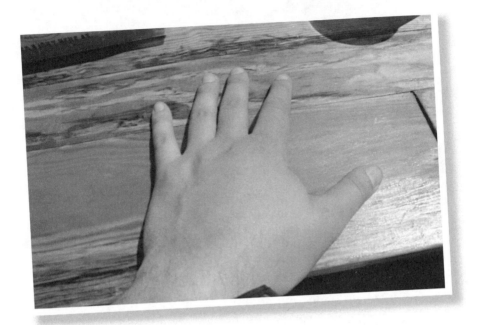

like Hellboy, but I could also barely get my hand through my shirt cuff. My Maine wilderness excursion had left me on edge, irritated, and ready to head the fuck back to Portland.

I say "back to Portland" because, having arrived in Maine a day or two early, I had had the good fortune to stay at the beautiful and expertly staffed Portland Harbor Hotel in the heart of the Old Port district. The rooms were exquisite and comfortable, well lit, and had doors that locked. In short, the diametric opposite of Abe Lincoln's house in South Casco, where I'd suffered at the expense of vampiric vermin.

My friend and I pulled off of the barely-wide-enough-for-one-car-let-alone-two dirt road leading out of town onto Route 302 (also known as the Roosevelt Trail) and headed due south with doors locked, A/C and tunes pumping, and the promise of civilization spurring us onward. As we drove south on 302, we began to see more frequent signs of civilization and fewer densely forested areas, but we were still clearly in vacationland.

Now, everyone knows that Maine is lobster country. Though hungry, I did not have the time, patience, or inclination at that moment to stop and eat a proper lobster dinner like the one I had had on my first night in Maine, at the legendary Lobster Shack at Two Lights in Cape Elizabeth. During that meal at the Lobster Shack, though, I'd tried something that I soon realized I'd only had pale approximations of before: the lobster roll.

A grilled Freihofer's roll is key to the experience. Also known as a New England–style hot dog roll, it's a hybrid of white-bread slices and hot dog buns. Into the bun go shredded lettuce and mounds of sweet, flaky (and clearly fresh) lobster claw and tail meat, all topped at one end with a half-dollar-size dollop of mayo and at the other with a pickle slice, and a dusting of paprika. Taking my cues from a Maine native at the next table, I removed the pickle, spread the mayo  over the whole thing, replaced the pickle, and took a bite.

If this book had a soundtrack, this is where a choir of angels would sing.

First off, the grilled New England roll was a total triumph. I had only sampled them previously with hot dogs, but they lend a decadent crunch to the first moment of the bite. The lettuce adds its own moist crunch. But then the creamy, smoky paprika-laden mayo touches the roof of your mouth and as you close your gob around the sandwich, the sweet, flaky-yet-chewy, still-moist-from-cooking and tasting-of-the-ocean lobster meat explodes in your mouth. It spins off into milky white strands like string cheese, at once a hearty mouthful, totally delicate, lowbrow and highbrow, and utterly perfect. The flavors develop further as you chew and work it around in your mouth, with the mayo melding with the meat and lettuce to create a mixture akin to seafood salad. The bun picks up flavor from the meat and pickle juice, not to mention the flavor it brought from the grill, making it a smoky, savory counterpoint to the refreshing lobster within.

It is a sandwich that, when done right, can be equal parts epicurean delight and straight-up comfort grub.

Taste-wise, it's proletarian and bourgeois all at the same time.

Sadly, price-wise it leans strongly toward the bourgeois, as it hovers around the ten-buck mark or better.

But I will say this, you cannot die without having had one (unless, of course, you are allergic, in which case you'll die *from* having had one. But what a way to go!). And make no mistake: Portland, Maine, is ground zero for the lobster roll experience.

Now, I need to say at the outset that I think Portland is awesome for many reasons. Until I went there to do the research for this book, what I knew of Maine was gleaned mostly from Stephen King novels and through the character "Hawkeye" Pierce on *M*A*S*H*, who was from Crab Apple Cove. I knew that its lobster was supposed to be the best and that there was a distinct maritime tradition. I knew that Michael Caine, as Dr. Wilbur Larch, wished the orphans in *The Cider House Rules* a good sleep with the benediction, "Good night, you princes of Maine, you kings of New England." I knew that those acquaintances and friends of mine who were well-off and sported cable-knit sweaters or Eddie Bauer footwear often vacationed there. In short, I knew Jack about Maine.

I am so glad I went.

When you picture Maine—not necessarily Portland, but the 23rd state as a whole—your go-to images are almost certainly maritime in nature: lighthouses, weathered sea captains, ships at harbor, and so on. More often than not they're also likely to be evocative of colonial America, or at the very least connected to that period through architecture or tradition. Of course, you picture that famously rocky, craggy, wooded coastline flecked with sea foam, tall pines, and granite jutting into the ocean, standing steadfast against whatever the North Atlantic and fate throw its way with the staid solemnity of Mount Rushmore.

At least that's what I envisioned.

And I wasn't entirely wrong.

But there is more to Maine, and way more to Portland.

Portland, at the southern end of Maine, is surprisingly hip and vibrant, with a growing live-music scene and an impressive food pedigree that is gaining major recognition. In fact, in 2009 *Bon Appétit* magazine named Portland the Foodiest Small Town in America.

Portland, Maine's largest city, is not its capital, though that assumption is a common mistake. It is arguably the state's most cosmopolitan city, if such a thing can be said about a city as laid-back and in touch with its past both culturally and architecturally as Portland is.

This relaxed nature is however, somewhat at odds with Portland's roots. Portland, in so very many ways, has been shaped by the slings and arrows that fate and nature have thrown its way, and it has inexplicably come out on the other side of geologic and historic impasses as one of the most significant tourist locations and hallmarks of natural beauty in the United States. Portland, survivor of four major fires, foreign raids, economic devastation, and the crushing wheel of industrial progress, bears as its crest a phoenix rising from the ashes; its motto is *resurgam*, which means "I shall rise again."

Geologically speaking, Maine is known for its breathtakingly dramatic coastline and especially for the heavily wooded areas that reach almost right up to the seashore. Its rocky cliffs, bays, and tidal pools and the myriad coastal islands that dot the landscape have provided artistic inspiration for everyone from Edna St. Vincent Millay to E. B. White.

But these very elements endure in the face of adversity, much like the people of Maine themselves. You see, Maine is an example of a drowned coast, the official definition of which is "a shoreline transformed from a hilly land surface to an archipelago of small islands after inundation by the sea." Valleys flood and become bays and inlets, and mountaintops and higher outcroppings along the coast become forested islands. The result is a one-of-a-kind coastline that has come to define the whole state in art, commerce, and culture. Flooding becomes beauty, and the biodiversity evident in the resulting marshes, pools, and bays is breathtaking.

Portland's climate is classified as humid continental. Its summers are often warm and humid, and winters can just suck. They are generally very cold, with frequent snowfall and persistent snow cover averaging 68 inches per season—totally oppressive to those not enamored of frigid weather. The area is actually in the middle-latitude temperate zone, where the weather can be erratic as cold polar air masses collide with warm tropical air masses. Because of this, climate-wise Portland actually shares more with Canada, upstate New York, and parts of Minnesota than with the rest of New England. Add to this the fact that Portland sits on a peninsula

Great Local Brews Worth Investigating

1. Racer 5 IPA—Bear Republic Brewing Company,
   Healdsburg, California
2. Spotted Cow Ale—New Glarus Brewing Company,
   New Glarus, Wisconsin
3. Christmas Ale—Great Lakes Brewing Company,
   Cleveland, Ohio
4. Allagash White—Allagash Brewing Company,
   Portland, Maine
5. Total Domination IPA—Ninkasi Brewing Company,
   Eugene, Oregon

and therefore is also subjected to the ravages of the water that surrounds it on three sides.

And yet, Maine not only manages to live up to the Vacationland moniker emblazoned on its license plates, but also sustains viable agriculture and aquaculture industries. Though forest-conservation efforts in the surrounding Maine woods have curtailed its once-thriving paper production activities, there is still a bustling fishing, oystering, and lobstering industry, and there are thriving pockets of potato, apple, and blueberry cultivation, too.

Not all of Maine's contributions to the table are edible; some are potable. Maine, much like Canada's eastern coast directly to the north, was formed largely by glacial activity, creating many mountain springs that now supply numerous bottled-water purveyors and local microbreweries, at least six of which are in Portland. (Allagash is freaking amazing, by the way.)

Portland's geography has also played a major role in its becoming a major cultural and culinary hub. Its location made it one of the East Coast's major port cities. As such, it served as the main entry point to the northeastern United States and the United States as a whole for many goods, services, and cultures, and soaked up influences from all over the world.

History did not make it easy for Portland's port to prosper. After being destroyed not once but twice within a 14-year span, Portland's port began to recover, only to be shelled almost out of existence by the Royal Navy in 1775 during the American Revolution.

After the war, the village on the peninsula, which had been called Falmouth, renamed itself Portland. It was an apt label, as the community became a vigorous port, though one that was relatively unheralded in its time. The port and the city's economy were hampered when the United States began having troubles with Britain again during the Embargo of 1807, which lasted just more than a year, and the War of 1812, at which time trade with the British was prohibited.

Years later, after joining the United States in 1820, Portland would rise to prominence as a port for Canadian exports that remained free of ice during winter months. A major railroad that connected Portland with Canada made the city a hub for new goods, both domestic and foreign. For a while, having the port and the rail terminus in Portland gave the city a major economic boost, and it became a stalwart in ship and locomotive building. However, fate once again dealt Portland a heavy fiscal blow when the train line was rerouted to make Nova Scotia the ice-free port of choice. Only when shipbuilding improved and ships became hardy enough to make the trek through the Northern Atlantic and inland Canadian ice floes did Portland rebound.

Today, there are still many boats, both charter and commer-

In 1851, Maine became the first state to ban alcohol except for "medicinal purposes." The Irish immigrant population, a major component of Maine's maritime and shipbuilding industries, perceived this ban as an attack on their culture (seriously) and formed a mob that rushed city hall, where they suspected Mayor Neal Dow was stashing liquor. (He was, though it was for medicinal use.) The violence that ensued became known as the Portland Rum Riot, and it ultimately led to a repeal of the ban. The moral: Never come between a Portlander and his booze.

cial, that carry on Maine's maritime tradition, and in 2005 the city's port was the 25th largest and the largest foreign inbound-transit port by cargo tonnage (way bigger than neighboring Boston) in the United States, as well as the largest oil port on the East Coast.

This reverence for the seafaring tradition is evident in Portland. Though the Artside district, which houses most of Portland's museums (like the Museum of Art), theaters, and historic homes, is on the rise and in the midst of a major revitalization, the Old Port district, with its proximity to the water, narrow cobblestone streets, boutiques, and restored buildings, is the place that really evokes the Maine of days gone by and glories past. It also houses some of the best restaurants in the city—and nearly 300 restaurants call Portland home.

Due to the state's relatively small population (Maine is the most sparsely populated US state east of the Mississippi River), the area is appealing to people who want to get away from their more hectic hometowns, including the "summer people" who come to Maine for its abundant fishing, sailing, and hiking opportunities and the "leaf peepers" who come in the fall. The more relaxed lifestyle and less-competitive restaurant scene have also drawn many chefs to Portland from nearby Boston and throughout New England. These chefs bring skills, flavors, and panache that they've picked up from cooking in major US dining cities and use them in a city that smells of salt air, has gorgeously restored cobblestone streets, and allows you to wear a ball cap and sneakers to dinner. It's a wonderful juxtaposition.

If Portland is Maine and Maine is lobster, by the associative property that is one of the few obscure mathematical concepts I have retained, it stands that Portland *is* lobster. This is true to an extent. But to mention only this drawn-butter beauty is to overlook so many of Portland's culinary wonders, including wild blueberries. Maine produces 25% of all wild (or "lowbush") blueberries in North America and is the largest producer of them in the world. Smaller than cultivated blueberries, these bright blue berries are Maine's official state fruit.

Portland's seafood palette also encompasses mollusks, often overlooked by tourists but revered by locals, especially clams. These appear throughout Portland restaurants in the form of clam cakes, fried clams or clam bellies, and, as ever, clams on the half shell, not to mention stews, soups, stoups, and fritters and whatever else Bubba from *Forrest Gump* used to say about shrimp. There are also fresh, flaky wonderful fish like cod, haddock, and halibut to be found in varied incarnations ranging from broils and boils to cakes and croquettes.

In this part of the world, much noise is made about the Italian

> The Italian sandwich got its name *not* from the historical origins of its main ingredients, but as a tribute by its creator, Giovanni Amato, to his homeland—Finland. (Just kidding, it was Italy.)

sandwich, the sub/grinder/hero/hoagie that hails from Portland. Giovanni Amato and his wife opened a little store on Portland's India Street in 1902 and began selling what is arguably one of the first Italian cold-cut subs. The sandwich itself is rather simple: Italian bread, salami, cheese, pickles, peppers, and some kind of oil dressing. While it's a solid, tasty sub, it's only really worth grabbing at one of its original locations, not at one of the myriad franchise locations that dot the New England landscape or at gas stations and convenience stores. Granted, I'm a New Yorker who's been eating deli fare in authentic, magnificent incarnations since I had teeth to chew with, so I acknowledge my potentially jaded, skewed perception of any "Italian" sandwich made outside of my favorite Brooklyn salumeria.

Not all of Portland's culinary tradition is savory. Another New England staple that I first encountered while in grad school in Connecticut is still ultraprevalent in Maine and nearly ubiquitous in Portland: the whoopie pie. A cream-filled cake sandwich thingy the size of a massive burger, whoopie pies are not unlike Drake's Devil Dog snack cakes, and they are utterly amazing. The filling is an inch- to two-inch-thick layer of vanilla and marshmallow fluff (usually in a suspension of vegetable shortening) sandwiched between two thick, moist cakes. Most often the cakes are chocolate, but red velvet and pumpkin variations are also popular. These sandwiches have their roots in regional Amish settlements and owe their name (according to

THE WHOOPIE PIE

legend) to the vocal reaction Amish men and children would have upon discovering one of these in their lunch boxes. It is ultradecadent, surprisingly light, and utterly insane. Delicious, decadent, and . . . I want one so badly right now. If you've had one, you know.

To properly finish off any account of Maine's contributions to our dining experience, I should add that Maine is the country's number one producer of toothpicks, to the tune of 20 million a day.

☆ ☆ ☆

But whoopie pies, blueberries, and other oceanic delicacies aside, coastal Maine is all about the lobster, and in particular the lobster roll, and with a free day and a rental car at my disposal and a willing tasting partner at my side, I resolved to spend the afternoon making a scientific survey of Maine's fabled sandwiches in all their delectable variety. With that in mind, my date and I hit the road.

Just south of the intersection of Routes 85 and 302, in the town of Raymond on the banks of Jordan Bay, we passed a triangular place with a striking red roof that went straight to the ground. The word "Lobsters" was displayed prominently on its roof.

We were hungry, we were curious, we made a right.

Upon pulling into the parking lot, we learned that the structure was, in fact, two connected establishments: the Fishermen's Catch seafood market and the Galley restaurant. And right there, on the Galley's sign, "Fresh Maine Lobster Rolls" were advertised. It is a seasonal place, open only from May to October, which not only made me feel psyched to have gotten a chance to be there, but also assured me of the freshness of the stock.

Now, any time I have ever encountered a place that is a combination market and restaurant, the food has been stellar. I have eaten steaks in stockyard restaurants and sushi in fish markets. This was going to be Maine's variation on the theme: lobster rolls made from the meat of lobsters sold under the same roof.

Upon entry, we found ourselves literally straddling the border between the market on the left and the bright, sunlit restaurant to our right.

I went to the market first, looking at lobsters swimming in open, wood-paneled tanks along the wall. The place was immaculate, devoid of that "fish smell," and I instantly felt good about eating what they had on offer. There were fresh fish inside a glass case with mussels, oysters, and littlenecks right beside them in neat little pyramids. And next to them I spied mounds of just-cooked fresh lobster meat sold by the pound!

Oh, hell yes!

I asked for an eighth of a pound, which was placed in a plastic baggie, and literally threw money at the poor dude behind the counter before running over to my date to share my spoils. We each reached in and grabbed a hunk of the fresh, succulent, red and ivory meat. She chose claw meat, I chose tail. We raised our lobster and toasted.

I can only explain the flavor this way: I tasted Maine. I tasted the ocean, the brine, the obvious care that went into getting the meat to this juicy, chewy, delicate state. I tasted the seaweed, the salinity of the ocean, the "lobstery" flavor imparted by the shell, the custardy sweetness found only in lobster at its freshest. The only thing I can compare it to is the king crab I once ate in Alaska.

As I chewed, I suddenly realized the obvious: *This is what they put in the lobster rolls.*

We made a beeline for the Galley restaurant, no more than a few steps from the live lobsters. It was bright and airy inside thanks to the floor-to-ceiling windows on the building's front and the vaulted roof. A young dude named Matt Sullivan, whose family owns the place and who's been working there since he was 14, and his wife, Megan, were in charge. They'd marked their location on a map of Maine with a piratelike *X*. A crusty old pirate dummy sat perched in the rafters. They were clearly having fun. Fun people often make the greatest grub.

We grabbed a menu.

And then the confusion set in. Yummy, delicious confusion.

The Galley has four different bread options for your lobster roll: plain, grilled with butter, oven toasted, or (be still my heart) garlic bread.

There are also four options for your lobster filling: Classic (light mayo), Butter Lovers (no mayo, just butter), Zesty Lemon (with lemon-pepper seasoning), and their signature Galley Roll (with sweet relish).

Four breads, four lobster fillings.

Do the math—I'll wait.

That's 16 different lobster roll possibilities.

Sixteen!

Luckily, we had two mouths to shoulder the workload, and we resolved to try at least four.

Yes, I was going to spend forty bucks on lobster rolls.

Don't judge me.

We chose the Classic both on grilled bread *and* on garlic bread (figured it'd be a solid contrast), the Zesty Lemon with grilled bread (love lemon and seafood), and since it is their signature dish, we decided to give the Galley Roll with grilled bread a shot.

The first we tried was the Classic. Absolutely sparkling fresh, it was very reminiscent of the one I'd had at Two Lights, although here the mayo was mixed in and there wasn't a ton of it, which I liked. They also used leaf lettuce rather than shredded iceberg, and this one had no pickle. It was a solid roll. Then we tried the Classic with garlic bread. Absolutely delicious. The savory, buttery crunch of the garlic bread was a rich contrast to the cold, sweet lobster chunks. The addition of that potent garlic flavor served as a canvas on which the lobster could shine. Next, we tried the Galley Roll. A

THE CLASSIC, WITH AND WITHOUT GARLIC BREAD

confetti-colored relish of greens and yellows dotted the white and red lobster meat. I took a bite. The relish was an incredible rush of flavor, absolutely delicious to be sure, but for me, it overwhelmed the lobster meat with its sharp, sweet, vinegary flavor.

The last one was not only my favorite, it was the best lobster roll I have ever eaten. Now, everyone knows that lemon and seafood go together like hugs and kisses, Starsky and Hutch, Kanye and controversy—and the Zesty Lemon roll proved the rule. The fact that it was lemon-*pepper* only made it better, as I find pepper cuts through the richness of everything creamy in a pleasant way, while the lemon made the already fresh lobster taste somehow fresher. The flavors remained explosive from first bite to last. The addition of just enough of the right seasoning made this lemon lobster roll truly a light, refreshing taste of summer with the heartiness of a heavier sandwich.

We left, happy as clams—or lobsters, or whatever—and headed farther south. And that's when it hit me. "I'm in Maine," I thought. "I do not know when or if I shall be back. If I'm gonna have a lobster roll experience, it'd better be here." And, remembering that the mere hour or so drive from where we were now to the Lobster Shack at Two Lights in Cape Elizabeth had showcased an intriguing number of variations on this magnificent sammie, I resolved to try every lobster roll on Route 302 back to Portland.

Every damn one.

I told my date. She rolled her eyes and laughed.

"Okay, Lobster Man. Let's do it."

Vroooom!

Just 5 or 10 minutes south, in North Windham, we came to Bob's Seafood, just west of Pettingill Pond near the Sebago Lake Basin. Like our previous stop, this was a seafood market as well as a restaurant, which is generally a good sign. We pulled over and walked into the long building with a lobster-festooned blue awning.

The menu was handwritten on a dry-erase board and additions were printed out on individual sheets of paper and taped to the board. I love the lo-fi, because more often than not with roadside spots, less money spent on signage, advertising, etc., usually translates into more spent on the food. As if to prove my point, on a little printed page near the ceiling I saw a picture of a lobster roll with the words "Lobster" and "Roll" written directly on the wall itself in red marker. I ordered one—just one—classic beauty. Belatedly, I saw a small sign on the pass shelf between the counter and kitchen that read, "Grilled Buns Available Upon Request." I nearly said something, seeing as how I had loved the grilled bun, but I ultimately decided, "Hey, if this is how Bob's does 'em, that's how I want it. I won't fool with their experience." A few minutes later, I got my lobster roll, swaddled in plastic wrap. We went outside and used the hood of my car as our dining table.

It bears noting that Bob's does *not* use the New England hot dog bun. They use a regular, old-school, white-flour hot dog bun. I unwrapped the roll, which was a *lot* more difficult than I thought it would be. It felt like a pastry to be honest, pillowy and soft.

I cannot lie. I instantly regretted the ungrilled bun. Not because the plain bun was inferior *in any way*, but because of the dimension I knew grilling had added to other rolls and because of my preference for the decadent *crunch-squish* you get when you bite into a buttery, grilled bun—a sensation heightened by the contours of a New England–style bun that, because it has crusty edges (like a slice of bread), when toasted develops the crispy corners we love.

I also prefer the firmness that toasted bread presents not only to the bite, but in the hand. I know it sounds weird, but for me, finger food, street food, handheld food, whatever you want to call it, needs to be as pleasing to the touch as it is to the tongue.

Think I'm alone in this? Think I'm weird?

Well, go back to the french fries you've eaten.

Don't limp, shitty fries feel shitty before you even eat them?

Don't those ultracrispy, sexy fries *feel* great before that first crunch?

I personally consider the tactile quality of handheld food to be one of its most overlooked dimensions. (And now I'll get off the soapbox.)

A generous amount of meat, more red than white, was coated with an ultrathin layer of mayo, just enough to give the lobster a sheen and hold the smaller bits together. From recollection and from looking at my photos, I'd say that Bob's used mainly claw meat, which isn't a bad thing, it's just that one particular texture of lobster meat was more prominent in the mouthfeel of this roll. There was no lettuce. There was no pickle. There was no pomp, circumstance, or pickle relish.

As I took a bite, I realized what the other dimension was that I missed from the sturdier grilled or toasted roll: It holds together when you bite it, whereas the soft roll collapses, smooshes, like the hot dog bun it is, causing the lobster meat—rich, expensive lobster meat—to spill everywhere.

The freshness of the lobster at Bob's was unassailable, but both my date and I found the lobster too *wet* somehow. It was almost soggy. Now, bear in mind this is lobster, so the baseline for it is delicious, but the absence of any flavor or texture other than watery, slightly lobstery, and soft, without any counterpoint like pickles, paprika, crunchy toast, or even lettuce, made this roll an okay but not great experience.

I'd come back to Bob's, but I'd be more inclined to try the ridonkulously good-looking fried clams the guy in line in front of me had ordered.

But the experience was eye-opening. I had not thought it would

be possible for a sandwich with such simple, amazing ingredients to be anything but stellar. I was wrong.

We left, feeling full—and a little disappointed. My date begged me to give up my quest to find the best lobster roll in southern Maine's vacationland corridor, but I was determined to try all I could, and to see the next change that a few more miles southward might bring.

Luckily she was a foodie, read the earnest look on my face, and decided to go along for the ride.

Now, I didn't try *all* the rolls I could have. We passed a Mickey D's on Route 302 that offered lobster rolls, but I'll be damned before I ever try what McDonald's might call lobster, and a diner that advertised a "Lobstah Roll" basket turned out not only not to have it, but to be staffed by some rude a-holes. But these were about the only exceptions.

Onward south we went, passing an amazing building covered with hundreds of hubcaps called Dick's Place. I still have no idea what it is.

In the town of Windham we stopped at a driving range to hit some golf balls and work off the lobster rolls. I instantly remembered why I love and hate golf, as I sliced the first three balls sharply to my right. Figuring that I'm a better eater than golfer, I marched back to the car to continue my search for stellar examples of Maine's finest. But I would have to soldier on alone if I found any more lobster places, as my date was stuffed. I was sad to lose the second opinion, and second tummy, but I pressed on.

Twenty minutes south, we were just outside of Portland in what seemed to be an Asian, or more specifically Thai and Vietnamese, neighborhood. We'd had time to digest a bit, and I hadn't passed a lobster roll purveyor in some time, so when we passed a little—and I do mean "little," like woodshed little—place on Forest Avenue (the southernmost appendage of 302) just outside of the city with a big white and red sign that read "Biggest Lobster Roll/Best Fried Clams Evah!" I pulled a U-ey.

The place, the Fishermen's Grill, was half of yet another market/restaurant combo (the market is called the Fishermen's Net). I was apprehensive as the place was virtually empty save for a ghetto-fabulous young Vietnamese couple, and it wasn't exactly what you'd call an attractive eatery, though it might be said to possess "character." It had black-and-white checkered floors, a small counter against the far wall, and a few tables.

Not knowing any better, I ordered a "jumbo" lobster roll, thinking it just meant a larger roll or more meat. When the large, shaved-headed man in the Patriots ball cap behind the register asked for nearly $20, I almost fainted. How big did it have to be to command *twice* the price of a regular roll? He replied, through the thickest New England accent, "You can get like two or three meals out of one of those."

"I'd just like a regular, please." The big dude rolled his eyes and told the chef, who was also wearing a Pats cap, that I'd "had second thoughts" and wanted a regular one, "the Classic."

My companion asked if he'd said "flaccid."

He laughed, we laughed—all was forgiven. There were no other patrons, so the chef immediately set about making my lobster roll.

While I could not see his hands, he did not stop working. And work he did for *several* minutes. My date made the astute observation that the amount of time and care that went into making just this one "regular"-size roll was a very good sign.

The roll was served in a white and red box, perched in a small cardboard sleeve inside. It was absolutely beautiful. The bread was toasted and slightly grilled, shreds of deep green lettuce poked out from beneath the filling, and mountains of claw and tail meat with a veneer of mayo were piled neatly in the center of the bun. In what was becoming a routine, we went out to the car to chow down, my date insisting that she couldn't eat a bite.

I took one bite and rolled my eyes in pure ecstasy. Once again, the delicious crunch of a perfectly grilled bun yielded to lettuce so fresh that it had flavor (!), not just crunch, and the lobster was perfect. Cold, firm, and yielding an explosive burst of juice when you bit into it. My date saw my reaction and said:

"Oh screw it, give me a bite." I did. She said, "That is amazing. I did not think I could eat any more and especially no more lobster, but that is just amazing." It was. The claw meat flaked and broke apart on my tongue as I chewed through the more meaty tail meat. Absolutely incredible.

She finished it, by the way.

On we continued into Portland proper, skirting the water's edge along Commercial Street in the Old Port district.

I drove a block past our hotel and pulled into a parking lot. "Adam, why are we stopping here?" asked my date. Then the realization washed over her. "Not another one!"

"Yup. Another one."

The one I had in mind was at the highly popular and more commercial Portland Lobster Company on Chandler's Wharf, a place so mainstream that it has indoor *and* outdoor seating, live music, and lobster-shaped pagers that buzz and light up when your order is ready. A far cry from the two-man operations of the Galley and Fishermen's Grill. Like the spot in the Beastie Boys' song "Paul Revere," the place was a-bumpin' and the girlies was hot. We waited on line, and I ordered the lobster roll that the *Portland Phoenix*'s readers voted the best lobster roll in Portland 2010. The menu describes it as "fresh picked meat from a one pound lobster, brushed with sweet butter. Served on a toasted roll with both mayonnaise and lemon on the side."

My date had officially thrown in the towel, but she assured me she could dig deep for one more bite.

The lobster roll arrived looking unlike any other roll we'd eaten, so already it was scoring points for originality. The ever-present roll was in this case crispy and crusty and perfect, and the lobster meat looked plump, pink, red, and ivory, though it was mixed with no mayonnaise at all. Beneath it were frilly, emerald curls of lettuce. Resting on top were two massive chunks of perfectly cooked claw meat, and covering everything was a translucent, bright yellow glaze of melted butter. Unlike previous rolls, this one came with fries (very good ones, at that) and coleslaw. Since I no longer had to drive, I ordered the formidably awesome local brew, Allagash, and sat down to my umpteenth lobster feast of the day.

I have to say this about the lobster at the award-winning, totally polished, packaged, and popular spot: It tasted like fine-dining lobster.

That is to say that rather than the "fresh cold seafood" taste of rolls previous, this tasted like the lobster from the "lobster dinners" I'd eaten with a plastic bib around my neck. It was delicious, and though it was mayo-less, not only did the presence of butter enhance the traditional lobster dinner taste, it did not interfere with amazingly cooked crustacean. Somehow, between the two of us we found room to devour the entire thing, along with the slaw (which was surprisingly good) and a good number of the very delish and crispy fries. Definitely a summer spot worth hitting again even if I'm not on the lobster-roll-a-palooza crusade.

We left, warm and very, very full.

"Adam," my date begged, "please, no more."

"One more."

"Really? Still?"

"One more."

And why the last one?

It was within walking distance and a previous Best Lobster Roll winner. It was at J's Oyster, on Commercial Wharf, one wharf east of Portland Lobster Company.

It's a substantial white structure with blue awnings, signage, and a roof that occupies the whole left side of Commercial Wharf. When you walk in, it's like a seaside Cheers: Where locals go. Where presumably everybody knows your name. Where people start drinking *early*. It looks more like a bar than a restaurant, which I totally dug, a bar bright with natural sunlight, but still a bar. No frills; all killer, no filler.

I ordered a lobster roll, my final one of the day, from the bartender, then went outside to wait. To kill time I tried to take artistic photos of an anchor at the end of the pier. Right about then, the avalanche of crustacean I'd ingested since leaving South Casco 25 miles northwest began to mount its assault. Suddenly, I wanted to go home. I wanted a nap. I wanted . . .

"Adam! Your order is up!"

Damn.

I dug deep and remembered my mantra: "Hey, when else am I gonna be in Maine to try this?"

I went in, paid the extremely nice counterwoman. And I do mean nice. When I walked in, I'd anticipated an unfriendly locals-only type of vibe from the staff. Not so at all. From the guy who took my order, to the lady who took my money, to the dude who brought out my food, they were all stellar. In fact, the only problem I had with the staff was the number of Boston Red Sox caps I saw, but hey, nobody's perfect.

I went back out into the parking lot amidst the seagulls and set my Styrofoam to-go box on a pylon and prepared for the last lobstery step of the journey.

The roll was grilled, and anointed with less butter than any I'd had so far. This made me optimistic because I figured that choice was based upon a desire not to obscure the pure flavor of the lobster itself. Full leaves of lettuce lined the roll, making the red lobster meat pop against the contrasting bright green. My order included ruffled potato chips and the most interesting accoutrement of all: a packet of Hellmann's mayo. Yup, my lobster was naked. I decided that if they didn't add it first, neither would I.

By this time, I admit it, I was pretty much lobstered out. So, poor J's was fighting an uphill battle.

I took my first mayo-less bite.

The meat was full of flavor and capital *F* fresh, but firmer and more crumbly than I prefer. I offered my date a bite. She took a small nibble and agreed that she, too, wanted slightly moister meat, but loved the huge leaves of lettuce and relatively dry bun around the meat because the fresh lobster flavor was so potent by contrast.

I added mayo and took another bite.

It tasted like very good and flavorful, albeit slightly dry, lobster with mayo squirted on top of it. End of story.

I was done.

We were done.

We absentmindedly picked at the lobster meat with our fingers and fed the chips and bun to the seagulls.

We'd eaten eight lobster rolls over the course of 25 miles and a few hours. And you know what?

I still love them.

Wet meat? Love it.

Dry meat? Love it.

Soft bun? Love it.

It's like getting some lovin'—even when it's bad, it's still damn good.

And Maine with its lumber and lighthouses will forever be our lobster capital. Its waters produce decadent deliciousness that can be enjoyed without a bib, a cracker, or drawn butter. That can be enjoyed while one holds a drink in the other hand. With meat that can change from succulent to so-so with one second more or less of cooking, that responds beautifully to subtle additions of flavor, whose texture and taste are entirely unique and can be transportive, orgasmic, and memorable.

The lobster roll, sandwich of sandwiches. Luxury and economy in a roll—a Bentley masquerading as a Subaru. It is a bite of the glorious, decadent, and expensive in a familiar, fun, and accessible package. It is as much a showcase for the lobster's versatility as it is for that of the chef who serves it. It shows how slight variations on a delicious theme can speak volumes. It is the fingerprint of a Maine seafood chef—the evocation of a unique identity, legitimacy, and connection to the legacy of rolls and fishermen long gone. It is a mouthful of Maine and a handful of heaven.

Start to finish, from blueberry pancakes at the legendary Becky's

Great Condiments from throughout the United States

1. Canceaux sauce—Portland, Maine
2. 3 A.M. Bobby Que Pepper Sauce—Bryan, Texas
3. Green sauce—Brasa, Minneapolis, Minnesota
4. Maple pesto—Press 195, Brooklyn, New York
5. Spicy BBQ Sauce—The Mean Pig BBQ, Cabot, Arkansas
6. Orange sauce for tacos—multiple locations, San Jose, California
7. Deluxe tomatillo sauce—Chuy's, Austin, Texas
8. Habañero sauce—Salt Lick BBQ, Driftwood, Texas
9. White Garlic Sauce—Zankou Chicken, Los Angeles, California
10. Macadamia Vanilla Bean Vinaigrette—Bern's Steakhouse, Tampa, Florida

My Favorite Lobster Rolls

Here, based entirely on my personal preferences and those of my travel companion, is a ranking of the rolls consumed during my Maine pilgrimage. There are some who will argue that one style or combination of ingredients is more traditional than another, that adding new or divergent flavors makes them inauthentic somehow. To them I say, if someone's ingenuity makes a dish delicious, then tradition be damned. Hockey was traditionally played without helmets; sometimes change is good (and prevents brain damage). And with no further ado, my lobster roll call.

1. Zesty Lemon with grilled bread—The Galley
2. The Classic—The Fishermen's Grill
3. Classic with garlic bread—The Galley
4. Lobster Roll (with butter and no mayo)—Portland Lobster Company
5. Lobster Roll—Lobster Shack at Two Lights
6. Classic with grilled bread—The Galley
7. The Galley Roll—The Galley
8. Lobster Roll (no mayo)—J's Oyster
9. Lobster Roll (dry, ungrilled bun)—Bob's Seafood

Diner, to lobster dinners at the Lobster Shack at Two Lights, to whoopie pies everywhere, to the toothpick that caps off the whole experience, Portland claps you to her granite bosom, shines her beacons of history and humility upon you, and grants you solace in the comfort foods of generations gone and yet to come.

Stand fast, ye princes of Maine! Ye kings of New England!

Bolstered against the waves crashing, standing steadfast at the bulwarks.

And remember Portland's municipal motto: I shall rise again.

Look up in the sky.

It's a bird.

It's a plane.

It's Portland-freakin-Maine.

Still here, dammit.

Weathered, wooded, and wonderful.

You should go.

Now.

GRILLED LOBSTER WITH BLUEBERRIES

Makes 2 servings

There are many, many lobster recipes. Those lovely bugs lend themselves and their delicious, usually very expensive meat to thousands of recipes—from the very fancy and labor intensive to the humble, easy, and unadorned. So rather than hit you with a slew of recipes, I'm gonna give you one of my favorite ways to cook lobster. On the grill. For a real taste of Maine, I serve this dish with Blueberry Mustard from the Moonshine Patio Bar & Grill (page 151). Even though that recipe comes from an Austin, Texas, restaurant, Maine is the only state in the United States that commercially grows wild blueberries, and the combination of blueberries and lobster is great!

> Two 1¼-pound lobsters
>
> Kosher salt and fresh cracked pepper
>
> 2 soft rolls
>
> 1 cup Blueberry Mustard (page 151)

To start, get your grill hot.

Then you've gotta kill the lobsters. (Yes, kill them. I love this cooking method, but to do it right, first you have to kill the lobsters.) The most humane way is to simply lay each lobster down on a cutting board right side up, the head toward you. Place the tip of a large knife about an inch or so behind the eyes and, in one motion, push the knife straight through the lobster till it hits the cutting board. Rock the blade down, splitting the front in half. This is painless and very quick for the lobster. Then flip the lobster over and split the tail using the same rocking motion.

Take the claws off and crack them enough to expose the meat, but DO NOT REMOVE THE MEAT OR SHELLS. Season the exposed tail meat and body cavity with the salt and pepper. (I also like using Old Bay Seasoning, celery salt, or lemon-pepper on occasion.)

Put the claws on the absolute hottest part of the grill. Add the tail meat and body cavity, and grill everything for 3 to 4 minutes. Flip and grill for another 4 minutes.

Remove from the grill and carefully pull the meat from the shell. Set aside.

Place the rolls on the grill and toast them, being careful not to burn them. Remove them from the grill and fill them with warm lobster meat. Top each with a dollop of the blueberry mustard.

CHAPTER 9

★ ★ ★

THUNDERBOLTS, BROKEN HEARTS, AND HEAT

★ ★ ★

SAVANNAH, GA

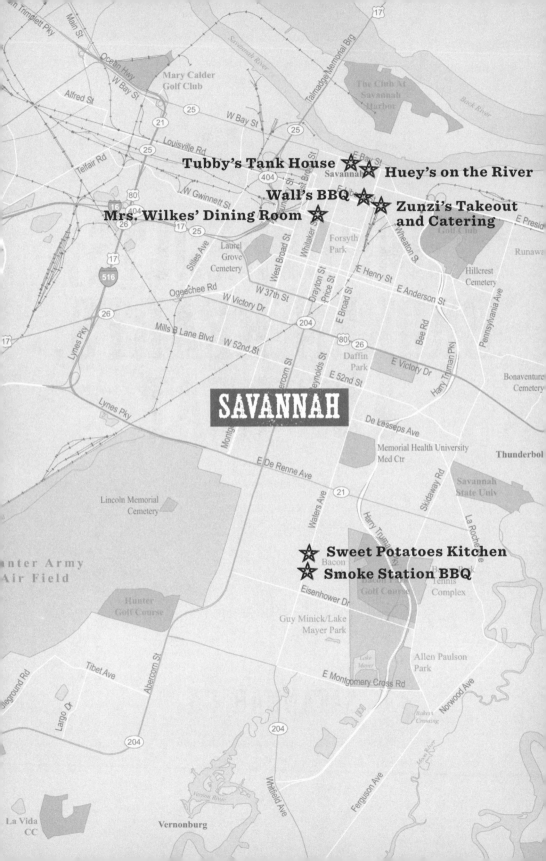

Tubby's Tank House

Huey's on the River

Wall's BBQ

Zunzi's Takeout and Catering

Mrs. Wilkes' Dining Room

SAVANNAH

Sweet Potatoes Kitchen

Smoke Station BBQ

Southern gothic writer Flannery O'Connor was born in Savannah, Georgia, on March 25, 1925. Her often grotesque antiheroes provide a hard-core image of real Southerners: flawed, but trying. Dimmed by darkness, hell-bent on reaching the light, in search of a divine grace they may have had all along.

Grace.

A concept that transcends religious doctrine and is subject to myriad interpretations. To me, it means salvation—and mercy for sinners.

I've sinned.

In O'Connor's stories, the characters often come to recognize their need for repentance and either accept or reject the opportunity. As I arrived in Savannah on a trip not all that long ago, I felt overcome by the need for change and a desire to find something lasting that would satisfy an appetite that had taken me from place to place, but constantly away from any meaningful connection, luring me into one doomed-from-the-start affair after another.

So my heart was heavy, my eyelids more so, as I headed through downtown Savannah. The tires, sticky on the black tar pavement, sounded like tape being torn off the roll as the light turned green. On this particular day, Savannah seemed like the hottest place on earth.

The hottest place anywhere.

At night.

By day.

Hot.

People smiled lazy Cheshire cat grins, their willowy limbs and spines swaying like the Spanish moss that hangs from nearly every tree as they walked along River Street in the 104°F heat.

I wilted and burned, from within and without. I looked heaven-ward for inspiration, but my feet were licked by flames. I was lost, tired, and overworked. I had escaped in search of some kind of a spark to focus me. The trick was getting out before that spark grew into an inferno that would consume me. I knew the drill.

I'd been here before.

I'd been here before, and I'd liked it. I like the steamy streets, the many little squares and parks that make the Historic District a one-way-street nightmare to drive in but utterly beautiful to walk through. I like the way a cold beer tastes here—and how too many beers feels there. I like that every woman here seems to know the inside joke, the dirty secret, and will never, ever tell. You can see it in their eyes: Maybe it's some ancient juju/hoodoo/voodoo thing that they share with one another, but these daughters of Eve, acclimated to the scorch of Savannah summers, have souls as old as the tides, freckles that spell out ancient constellations, and unendurably short shorts. The men are born of oak and hickory shaped by rivers, wind, rain, and the legacy of General William Sherman (for better or worse), which combine to harden up hands, hearts, and torsos. And these sirens of the Southern Seine, furies of the floodplains, weave their warm, whiskey spell round them. All the while, Savan-nah burns. Like I said, I'd been here before.

Hungry from the hours of travel and nostalgic for the flavors of the state where I'd lived for six years as a student in Atlanta, I set off in search of barbecue. Local stalwart Walls' Bar-b-que was closed for the season, so I headed to a place outside the thick of Savannah called Smoke Station BBQ, a barn-red building with a massive smoker and thick hunks of wood piled out back. This place uses only woods from nut-bearing trees, giving the smoke exceptional flavor.

It was just after the lunch rush, so the place was mostly empty.

Georgia coastal barbecue is similar to Western North Carolina barbecue in that it is largely made with only the pork shoulder, smoked with hardwoods or fruit-woods, prepped with a flavorful rub, and slathered with a thicker, tomato-based sweet hot sauce.

I grabbed a corner table and basked in the delicious recirculated air-conditioning. The waitress had a thousand-watt smile and treated me like a friend she'd been waiting to catch up with; from the first "honey" out of her mouth, I was smitten. She brought me an iced tea, and when I asked what to order, she told me, "Whatever you do, get our burnt end pork, it's just like the best meat we've got, all crunchy and chewy." She recommended the sandwich, advertised on the menu as "a real man's sandwich," but while I fancy myself as real as the next guy, I wanted to try more than one meat to see how they each reacted to the smoke, so instead I went with a two-meat combo plate with burnt end pork and beef brisket. (I always prefer to go with a plate rather than a sandwich at barbecue spots because you get a better sense of the pure meat flavor; a combo platter lets me try the pit master's skill across the board and provides a great background for experimenting with sauces.) I followed my waitress's suggestion on the sides: mac and cheese ("like my granny's—homemade") and some vinegar-based coleslaw. And just because I almost never get to eat them anywhere *but* Georgia, I added some fried green tomatoes to my order.

I waited for my food with a weary head full of thoughts. Too much road. Too much on my plate. Too much chagrin at some of the stuff I'd been up to, knowing I'd been raised better. Knowing I'd let myself down a couple of times. Knowing any hopes for something lasting

Five Great Side Dishes

1. Tomato pudding—Hominy Grill, Charleston, SC
2. Guacamole, spinach (tied)—Brasa, Minneapolis, Minnesota
3. Mac-n-Cheese—Slows Bar-B-Q, Detroit, Michigan
4. Roasted corn relish—Moonshine Patio Bar and Grill, Austin, Texas
5. Hummus—Sahadi's, Brooklyn, New York

with a couple of good ladies were lost to me forever because of choices I'd made and the "tyranny of distance" (thanks to rocker Ted Leo for that turn of phrase, the title of his second album). But I was here to right that course.

Thankfully the tomatoes came to distract me from my reveries, and thankfully they were amazing, the breading crisp but not at all oily and dotted with black pepper, the tomatoes tart and firm fleshed. I all but inhaled them. The void in my stomach somewhat appeased, I sat back, sipped my tea, and promised myself that this time around things would be different, better, sharper.

The lovely waitress with the megawatt smile and country gravy curves returned with a plate of redolent, smoky barbecue in her hands. Lawd, Lawd, Lawd—girl, take me now and help me get my mind right. The brisket was juicy, and its overt meatiness reminded me of prime rib. Delicious, but the waitress was right—the pork was incredible. It was smokier than I expected, but not overly so, and the charred bits from the outside of the butt contrasted in a delectable way with the juicier bits from the meat closer to the bone. The mac and cheese was not creamy, but rather

more like small elbows of macaroni with nice, little crispy bits of cheese baked onto it, and the vinegary slaw cut right through all the rich food. Topping it all off were Smoke Station's thick, tomato-based sauces, which are justly lauded for their balance of sweet and heat. (I also love the fact that they are served in the kind of slide-top dispensers IHOP uses for syrup). All had a rich sweetness that gave way to the bite of pepper on the back end, and the unctuous meat toned down the heat just enough.

Without asking, my wonderful waitress brought me an ice-cold iced tea to-go and a warm farewell with my check, and I was on my way.

Back in town, I headed toward the river, toward my hotel, sweating that slow, steady ooze of perspiration that comes when you're already moving slowly and the Southern air just coaxes the water out of you. I could hear peals of music from Congress Street and saw strapping young lads heading toward clusters of tan-legged, sway-backed, sun-dressed recipes for exquisite disaster. And who was I to judge? I myself was in thrall to more than just Savannah's juke joints, juleps, and sinfully good home cookin'.

And she was headed over to my hotel.

We'd met on an otherwise inauspicious night many years past, when college and circumstance had me in Georgia and happenstance had us crossing the same street at the same time. Two bars and an impromptu hotel room later, we were a tangle of gnashed teeth, white knuckles, and throaty gasps of humid, magnolia-scented air.

We'd kept in touch.

I braced for the arrival of this switchblade-sexy rockabilly baby who couldn't have weighed more than 105 pounds yet flattened me like a 17-ton tidal wave. Experience had taught me that she was twice as unpredictable as a tsunami, and capable of far more damage. Her sudden, summer-storm flashes of passion or petulance captivated me completely, her reactions a flurry of tattoos and coal-black eyeliner, hairpins, and histrionics. She made me a lion, and for sport would slaughter me like a lamb. And I bled out into a bourbon glass at bars along Bay Street, loving every frustrating minute of it.

If I was seeking grace, I had come to the wrong place, it would seem.

She arrived looking like someone who should be painted on the nose cone of a World War II bomber. Her eyes reduced me to ash as if not a single day had passed since we'd first met. She said, "Hey, boo," and the protective barricades I had erected between us collapsed. I kissed her like her lipstick was the antidote, she curled her calf 'round mine.

That was all it took.

Later, gazing up at the slow waltz of the ceiling fan, we began to work backward through small talk to catch up. And then everything began to darken as the flames rose around us. One misunderstood phrase gave way to another as the abscesses of little, unspoken problems that time and distance had allowed to fester into full-grown malignancies began to assert themselves.

"Let's just try to start fresh tomorrow," she said.

"You're leaving?"

She smiled, amused at my frustration, I think. "I could stay if you want. But that is if you want."

"Good Lord, I'm not the one heading for the door—I'm the one asking you to stay."

"Are you?"

"Huh?"

"Are you asking me to stay?"

"Yesss," I rumbled through clenched teeth. And with that, as if nothing had happened, she jumped in bed and curled up next to me.

"I have to wake up and head home early. But let's meet for lunch. So good to see you again." She gave me a quick kiss and shut her eyes.

I stayed frozen in what-the-fuckdom, staring at her incredulously, as she fell asleep beside me.

I stared at the ceiling, knowing that this shouldn't be so hard, and eventually fell asleep. And woke up alone, in the hottest room in the hottest town on earth.

As a Jew in the Deep South, I take comfort in the fact that Savannah has long been a refuge for the outcast. Forty-two Sephardic Jews fleeing the Spanish Inquisition in Spain and Portugal arrived in Savannah in 1733, just five months after English colonists had established the settlement under General James Oglethorpe. Thanks to the advocacy and leadership of Oglethorpe, these Jewish immigrants were allowed to settle in the colony of Georgia, and they would go on to establish the first Jewish congregation in the South. Savannah's need to attract residents (if not necessarily a sweeping tolerance for religious diversity) led the leadership also to grant entry to groups of Greek Orthodox immigrants, as well as to Irish and French Catholics and Huguenots.

Some historians consider the citizens of Savannah's overwhelming rejection of Anglican pro-Crown theology and the Church of England in favor of Protestant beliefs (including such tenets as freedom and equality of all men before God) a precursor to the Revolutionary War. Another of those Protestant principles: a moral imperative to rebel against tyrants.

During the Revolutionary War, Savannah came under British and loyalist control, and in 1779 it was the site of a battle that cost the lives of more than 750 French and American soldiers in a failed attempt to recapture the city. In 1782, Savannah was freed of British rule and the city began to flourish.

In the 19th century, the Port of Savannah became one of the most active and culturally vital ports in the United States. Savannah's residents had first dibs on the wide array of fine goods arriving from foreign merchants, and in a lucrative game of turnabout, any goods produced stateside had to go through Atlantic ports like Savannah's before they could reach Western Europe.

For a relatively tiny city, Savannah was a *very* rich one, exporting a small fortune in goods (to the tune of $14 million by 1820). It is important to recognize, however, that this wealth came to Savannah as a result of both the removal of the indigenous peoples from the interior of Georgia to make room for green-seed cotton crops and the ever-growing slave trade. Savannah not only was a receiving point for slaves from Africa, but also was the site of this country's largest slave auction.

But Savannah was not spared from misfortune. In 1820, a fire left nearly half of the town in ashes, but residents rebuilt. That same year also saw an outbreak of yellow fever that killed a tenth of its population.

During the Civil War, the city's economy was devastated by strict sea blockades that severely hampered trade. Still, Savannah was a prized city. When General Sherman captured Savannah, he was said to have been so impressed by its beauty that he could not destroy it. In a December 22, 1864, telegram to President Abraham Lincoln, Sherman offered the city to him as a Christmas present. After the war, many freed slaves flocked to Savannah and would become a vital part of the city's economy and culture.

Today, the Port of Savannah is still one of the city's major economic powerhouses as well as a crucial factor in the regional cuisine, providing access to a variety of incredible seafood as well as ingredients and foodstuffs from abroad.

Foodwise, Savannah is a blissful blend of a port city on a river, a Southern home-cookin' icon, and the region's closest facsimile to New Orleans. But when you're talking Savannah cuisine, it all

For history buffs, Savannah is a wet dream. I'm serious. From architecture, to trails, to artifacts and restored buildings, the past is totally present in Savannah. I challenge anyone to sit on a bench in one of the 22 lush, quiet, tree-lined and grass-layered squares set amidst the thick, drooping greenery and two-story Victorian homes of the historic district and not feel totally transported to antebellum days.

really comes down to two things: shrimp and barbecue. Those are two of my favorite things, and Savannah truly has some of the best barbecue to be had, which is another way of saying it's some of the best food on earth. But of course that's not what had brought me here.

The next morning, confused and slightly on edge—but very hungry and ready for some Savannah savory to make it all better—I phoned and we resolved to meet at Mrs. Wilkes' Dining Room, the famous lunch counter on Jones Street that has been serving legendary home cooking since the early '40s. The place opened at 11 am, and when we met up at 11:20, the line was already down the block and around the corner. I asked a stopped pedi-cab driver how long he thought our wait would be, and he estimated an hour and a half to two hours.

"Do you wanna wait?" she asked.

"Hell and no."

"Let's go to Zunzi's."

"What's a Zunzi?"

Zunzi's, as it turned out, is a South Africa–themed takeaway eatery with a tiny counter and some outdoor seating with bright umbrellas. It wasn't too far away from Mrs. Wilkes', located on York at Drayton Street, a block from yet another beautiful green, shady public square.

The fact that I was eating South African fare in a place that, much like South Africa itself, once had sharp divisions between its black and white citizenry did not escape me and, to be truthful, it intrigued me.

As we walked up, she noted that it was rare for this place to have no line and informed me that, if I were smart, I would get the amazing Conquistador chicken sandwich. Of course I didn't, but she did, and it did look great: a baguette filled with shredded chicken pulled from a fresh-cooked breast right in front of you and topped with their super-special secret sauces (which vaguely reminded me of Caesar and Russian or Louis dressings, but with a hint of curry). I tried a bite and it was superb, perhaps the juiciest chicken sandwich I've ever eaten; one needed not a napkin but a tarpaulin to control the succulent overflow of the natural juices of the chicken and secret sauces. I went with the antagonistically named Boerewors on a Roll, a special South African–style sausage dressed with thick gravy and mustard, also in a baguette. The woman running the kitchen was rather insistent that I try the sausage before my sandwich was made, as she said it was "a particular taste that not everybody likes." I wasn't everybody. It crumbled like chopped meat, and the taste reminded me of a curried meat pie.

We grabbed our food and sat down at one of the tables outside under an umbrella working valiantly to ward off the unrelenting assault of the sun. I looked at this inked, wild, wonderful creature with me, and as much as I was trying to be present with her, I kept going back to the unexpected drama of the night before—and her ability to act as though it had never happened. I hovered above the

Boerewors is made from coarsely minced beef (sometimes combined with minced pork, lamb, or both) and spices, usually toasted coriander seed, black pepper, nutmeg, cloves, and allspice. (Thanks, Wikipedia.)

meal like a neurosis-addled specter, waiting for a resolution that seemed destined never to come.

The sandwich oozed as I bit into the baguette, the meat crumbling and mixing with the silky gravy. The mustard bit back very nicely. And my beverage? South African Rooibos iced tea. Yup, a barbecue sandwich and iced tea, African style, in a place once connected so cruelly with that distant continent but that now celebrates its cuisine.

The meal was good, helping me to focus on what I needed to do—namely, read the writing on the wall and walk away from a situation that perpetually careened ahead at Mach 3. This woman

South Africa does in fact have a barbecue tradition, called *braai*. A braai is a social gathering centered on grilled meats, and it has specific unspoken rules and observances. According to both black and white South African culture (thank you to my South African friends who taught me all of this), women rarely grill meat at a braai because it is considered a man's job. And not even all the men; there is traditionally one dude in charge of the whole shebang—fire, meat, coals, you name it—while the women make the salads and side dishes. The rest of the guys in attendance can help, but generally they just talk to the main braaier while he grills.

Sound familiar?

is sexy and smart, and had I as many arms as Shiva, I still could not cope with the handful she is. My mind reeled when I looked in her eyes, but I never once saw forever there, and it was time to look for one. And though, like Jimi said, I wanted to stand next to her fire, I just couldn't take the heat. I needed to man up and walk out. I needed to confront this head-on, I . . .

"I have to head home and get ready for a work commitment," she said.

"No problem, I have tons of stuff to do. You need a ride?"

"No, I can walk."

And we kissed the last kiss we would ever kiss.

Deflated, angry, but beneath it all perhaps just a bit relieved, I got in my car and gunned it toward the sea, toward the shrimping town of Thunderbolt, Georgia, and the islands that make up the Savannah coastline, somehow less encumbered than I'd felt in a long while.

Just before town, I pulled off by the bridge and sat on a pier watching the boats for a long time. I rather suddenly realized that the opportunity to eat shrimp in a modern shrimping town is not only a special thing, but also an increasingly rare one in light of the decimated seafood industries of the Gulf Coast, courtesy of BP's Deepwater Horizon Platform belching gallons of crude all over the American dining landscape for years to come.

Thunderbolt got its name from a lightning strike that allegedly created a freshwater spring on the bluff over the Wilmington River. It was a shipping port for local plantations and also serviced river traffic. The town was incorporated in 1856 and became a processing port for Georgia fishermen. Today, Thunderbolt is a major player in the state's shrimping industry. Nearly everywhere in town are docks for working shrimp trawlers.

Despite being only five miles removed from downtown Savannah, the two towns' ratios of African American residents to whites are almost completely reversed.

I cruised along the waterway and came to a joint that looked like it had seen better days a long time ago, if it had ever seen them at all. A sign promised barbecue and seafood, and shrimp seemed to be a specialty. Boats docked feet away from the door suggested the ingredients would at the very least be fresh, and experience has shown me that very often these little places that look downright shady have the best, most straightforward and unadorned food. No question, this place was indeed shady. Not just the ramshackle surroundings, not just the crappy signage and random pieces of equipment that littered the front, but even the employees struck me as sketchy. Two guys in particular looked like the methiest meth heads that ever methed. But hey, I wasn't there to judge, I was there to eat.

I entered the ultra-no-frills store and ordered the shrimp, opting for no fries, just shrimp. The man behind the counter assured me that "Shrimp is runnin' great now. Reeaaal good." I waited for my food in the downright funky kitchen, nervously checking that my Star of David necklace was covered whenever one of the suspect workers walked by. I was eventually handed a surprisingly heavy Styrofoam container brimming with golden fried shrimp and took it out to my car to eat.

I opened the box on my roof and was immediately impressed by the bang-for-the-buck quotient, but at this point I was getting a strong *Deliverance* vibe and I mostly just wanted to eat quickly and get the hell out of Dodge. The shrimp had a fresh, briny taste and were fairly succulent for such tiny creatures, but overall they were on the rubbery side, and the visible streak of shrimp shit running down the undeveined back of each detracted from the flavor and psychological appeal of the dish. Knowing I was eating in seemingly hostile environs convinced me to cut my losses, hop in my car, and head for a cleaner, more user-friendly shrimp shack, having learned a valuable lesson: Sometimes a dive is a gem, and sometimes it's just a dive. Don't be afraid to admit to your mistakes and move on.

And lo and freakin' behold, down the road I came across Tubby's Tank House, a clean, friendly, fun-looking spot. I'd heard about Tubby's back in the day from a guy at a bait shop who'd told me that the shrimp-boat guys not only regularly sell their fresh catches to Tubby's, but also eat there themselves. I pulled into the lot of a large shanty and grabbed a seat at the nautical-themed bar.

There were a few patrons, nearly all male and easily 15 to 20 years my senior. The sole bartender was a very attractive blonde in a sundress I'm sure she regretted wearing around the lecherous assembly.

I asked her how fresh the shrimp were.

"We get 'em from a fisherman next door."

I mentioned my last stop cautiously, asking if that were the source of their seafood.

"Eww. No. But they're delicious and so is the tuna. Crazy fresh."

"I'll do a little plate of each."

The shrimp arrived in a martini glass, a twee affectation that bummed me out, but after a bite all was forgiven. These shrimp were clean; had been boiled in some vat of spicy, savory, saffron-colored deliciousness; and were plump and juicy. The tuna, though as fresh as advertised, was unremarkable when stacked against the luscious shrimp. I ate in silence, slowly falling back into myself.

As I watched the patrons make passes both skillful and clumsy at the sweet blonde behind the bar, I felt myself growing disgusted, both because I could sense how uncomfortable it was making her and because, sadly, I saw echoes of my own past in the conduct of these past-their-primates. At this point in my life I wanted more—from myself, for myself.

I drove back into town and went to the cobblestoned, trafficked thorough-fare alongside the Savannah River that is Factors Walk, by River Street, eager to lose myself in something louder than the nonsense in my own head. The caw-ing of gulls, the laughter of children, and the brassy report of a trombone along the river imparted a sense of calm, yet there was also a sense of geographic confusion. The tiered, terraced homes, the omnipres-ent shrimping industry, even the jazz being played along the river-bank all brought to mind New Orleans. Maybe a slice of the Big Easy would provide the answer to my big difficulties.

I plopped myself down at a table outside of a N'awlins-style eatery called Huey's, right on River Street. And as I listened to the "wahhh-wahhh" of a nearby trombone, I ordered beignets and café au lait and for a moment fancied myself in another city also criss-crossed by canals and pummeled by storms and hurricanes. The beignets were funnel-cake rich, airy, crunchy, and sweet, and in

Savannah is like N'awlins in that it:

- is prone to flooding
- relies on a system of canals to control water flow
- is prone to hurricanes
- is a port city (and was a major port of entry for the slave trade)
- has a major shrimping industry
- has a population that's more than 50% African American, a percentage of whom are Gullah people, descendants of slaves from Sierra Leone who brought the practices of voodoo or hoodoo with them

In fact, in the popular Savannah-set story *Midnight in the Garden of Good and Evil*, the "midnight" in the title refers to the period between the time for good magic and the time for evil magic, a hoodoo notion.

that brief moment of reflection I realized as much as I loved it there, it was not where I should be.

I needed to leave town. I needed to leave her. Moreover, I needed to be alone. I could not plant a flag in unstable soil. Time and heat had warped the puzzle, and the pieces just didn't fit anymore. Maybe I'd come back when I could stand the heat, or maybe I'd find someone else to keep me warm.

I called her, told her my heart, which she characteristically turned back on me, spitting venomous little darts in an effort to hurt me in return. But the torpid weather had turned me to vapor. and the spite and spit passed through me like heat waves.

It was done. We were done. I jumped in the car and made a break for it.

I didn't blame Savannah. I still don't. I think the steamy environment there just peels back our armor, revealing the tender, fleshy parts that can caress or kill us, and gives us the tools to do both. I will always love Savannah, if not for the heat of its passionate soul, for the warmth of its passionate heart.

And, as if on cue, I passed by Sweet Potatoes, a place on the road out of town that claims to serve "endearing food." Once again I walked into a mostly empty blissfully air-conditioned room. A hipsterrific waiter strode across the festively painted dining room (which looked like a cool little-kids' classroom) to take my order. A friend had recommended their barbecued chicken with peach glaze, and at the waiter's suggestion, I went for corn pudding and green beans to go alongside.

I can't tell you how good I felt just sitting there, no fights, no heat. I was cooling off and keeping my cool.

My meal came, a perfectly roasted piece of chicken with a crisp skin and a small dish of homemade, chutneylike peach glaze accompanied by a slab of light, quichelike corn pudding and bacony, fresh green beans. The glaze was thick enough to coat the chicken, but thin enough to allow it to be seen and tasted. The meal was stellar in its simplicity and artful execution. The music was upbeat. Things were centering, and I found myself suddenly becoming good company *to myself*. I decided to treat myself . . . to dessert.

Which is how I stumbled onto what is without exaggeration the very best banana pudding I have ever tasted. It was a thick, creamy, cakey bowl filled with chunks of banana, vanilla wafer cookies, and

Great Desserts of My Life

1. Banana pudding—Sweet Potatoes, Savannah

2. Horchata fudge—Oooooooh ... FUDGE, Westside Market, Cleveland, Ohio

3. Sweet and salty cupcakes—Baked, Brooklyn, New York

4. Mint chocolate chip ice cream—Chocolate Room, Brooklyn

5. Banana pudding—Austin Gourmet Pudding, Austin, Texas

6. Key lime pie tart—Berns Steak House, Tampa, Florida

7. Chocolate haupia pie—Ted's Bakery, Haleiwa, Hawaii

8. Pumpkin pie concrete—Ted Drewes Frozen Custard, St. Louis, Missouri

9. Peanut butter and jelly cupcakes—Hill Country, New York, New York

10. Original cheesecake, plain (toppings are for pussies)—Junior's, Brooklyn

11. Butterscotch pie—Yoder's, Sarasota, Florida

12. Handmade marshmallows, or sweet almond bread pudding—Sweet Melissa Patisserie, Brooklyn

13. Snikkers ice cream—Emack and Bolio, Boston, Massachusetts

14. Berries and cream cake—Urth Caffé, Los Angeles, California

15. Memphis Mafia fritter—Voodoo Donut, Portland, Oregon

233

thick, custardy pudding that achieved the sense of blissful balance that I myself sought. It was light, yet rich without being cloying. It was, in my opinion, the edible manifestation of divine grace. It was a fitting end to the meal that saved Savannah for me. It was a hug, a pat on the back, a smile from a familiar friend who'd missed me. It was my meal—full of love, light, promise, and passion—that I ate alone, no date, darling, or debutante. Just me, myself, and I.

I'd come to Savannah knowing I needed something. Knowing I was lost and looking. Grasping at something as ephemeral as the heat waves snaking off the pavement. Like a Flannery O'Connor character I may never achieve grace, but like them my eyes are ever cast heavenward. And I saw that the salvation and the solidity I sought was not to be found in any relationship, shrimping town or sandwich. It was being my own love affair and my own company. There was true grace in enjoying a simple meal, in an otherwise empty dining room, finding comfort in myself as the Southern heat dissipated into the night. And it was there, alone but not lonely, by myself but not selfish, that I began to feel a sense of calm, love, and equilibrium. It was there that I laid down my arms, stopped running and opened myself up to Savannah and salvation.

I'm inclined to agree. No timpani, no pomp. Just me, my hopes, my prospects, my fork, and my knife. I'm not sure I know yet what I need, but I know this: The soul will always persevere in its search for quiet, bedrock, a home, and it is resilient.

And as I pulled out of the parking lot and roared out onto the highway, just beyond the fireball dropping below the horizon I caught a shimmering glimpse of something I'd been unable to find in any dish, in any bed, in any city, in any momentary pleasure. There, stretched out before me, waiting for me as though it had always been:

Grace.

THE 2ND BEST BANANA PUDDING

Makes 6–8 servings

The most incredible banana pudding I've ever had was at Savannah's Sweet Potatoes restaurant. When I can't get down there, I have a recipe that comes damn close. It's easy to make, but you need to do it in a few stages, with two different periods of waiting for the pudding to transform into deliciousness in the refrigerator. So it's best to start the pudding early on the day you want to serve it.

  1 can (14 ounces) sweetened condensed milk

  1 box (3.4 ounces) instant vanilla pudding

  3 cups heavy cream

  1 box (12 ounces) vanilla wafers

  4 cups sliced ripe bananas

In a bowl, whisk the condensed milk together with 1½ cups water. Add the pudding mix and whisk briskly for about 2 minutes. Cover and refrigerate for 4 hours or overnight. (Don't continue the recipe until the pudding mixture is set.)

In a large bowl, use an electric mixer on medium speed to whip the heavy cream until stiff peaks form. Fold the pudding mixture into the whipped cream with a rubber spatula, mixing gently until well blended and no streaks of pudding remain.

Cover the bottom of a large glass bowl with about one-third of the wafers, overlapping if necessary, then top with one-third of the bananas and one-third of the pudding mixture. Repeat the layering twice more, garnishing the top with a few reserved wafers or wafer crumbs. Cover tightly with plastic wrap and refrigerate for 4 hours—but no longer than 8 hours—before serving.

CHAPTER 10

★ ★ ★

A LEFT-COAST LIFE, PART II

★ ★ ★

LOS ANGELES, LA

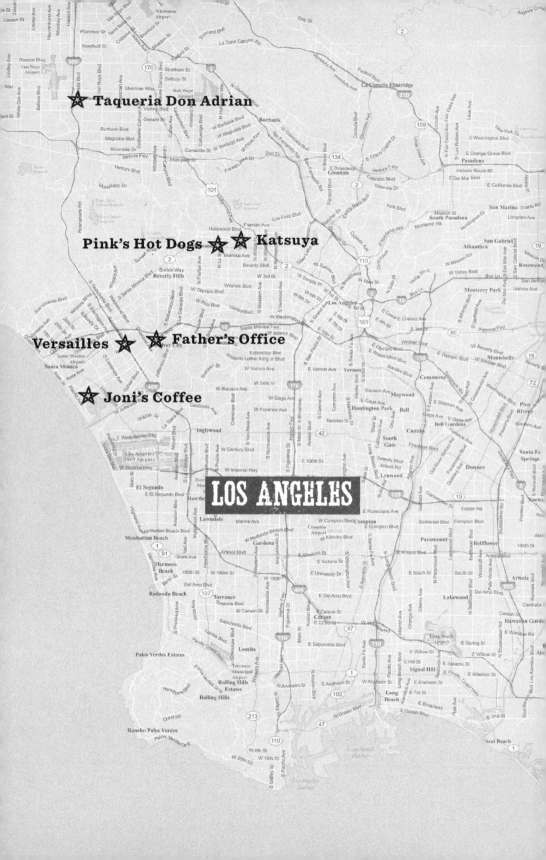

Taqueria Don Adrian

Pink's Hot Dogs ⭐ ⭐ Katsuya

Versailles ⭐ ⭐ Father's Office

⭐ Joni's Coffee

LOS ANGELES

It is morning. It is 2009.

I wake up in a suite in a Beverly Hills hotel.

I have a slight hangover headache.

I am naked.

Lying beside me is a beautiful woman with a warm heart, and a warmer body.

I am back in Los Angeles.

I am no longer auditioning.

I am "a name."

I am rested and resting.

I roll over and call in to do an interview with a magazine while the woman beside me rests her head on my chest and murmurs softly. I smile.

I go back to sleep.

We awake a few hours later.

Make love like I am about to head off to war.

Shower.

And leave in separate cars.

Realizing how hungry I was, I headed west to Joni's, an old-favorite breakfast spot near my first-ever LA residence in Marina del Rey. Known for its coffee, Joni's has been around since the 1980s, serving as much food that fits gym junkies (six egg whites, chicken, and veggies) as straight-up comfort food. I went for what I always order: huevos rancheros with three perfectly cooked eggs, purpley indigo black beans, and unrelentingly fresh, kryptonite green guacamole. But the star at Joni's was, is, and always will be the coffee.

Joni's coffee is very much like Joni herself—fun, fun-loving, occasionally cowboy-hat wearing, and completely original. A mammoth roaster that looks not unlike a massive steam engine is right inside the restaurant, and the coffee is made with what they call "lean osmosis water." Having looked that up, I learned that it likely refers to what results from the process of purifying water by pushing it through a membrane to remove organic contaminants. The result is very good. Each order is poured through its own filter and drips right into the cup. Feel free to read that again: *Each cup is filtered individually.*

I grabbed a seat outside behind the restaurant, allowed my coffee to settle, rubbed my eyes, and thought about the day ahead and the night before.

I thought about sitting at this same exact table six years earlier, pissing and moaning about a breakup and coming to terms with the fact that the girl had moved on well before I had. And then I sipped the coffee. It was deep, dark ocher and wonderful. It smelled of the roast, it tasted of hillsides and peat, and it was exactly what you want a great cup of coffee to be.

The waitress brought out my breakfast, and the smell of the beans and the sight of the fresh Cali avocado were like red capes to a bull. I charged. And with an appetite fueled by wantan lovemaking and nostalgia (Joni herself recommended this dish to me ages ago), I laid waste to the dish.

The eggs were fluffy and devoid of unnecessary grease or butter. The beans had just enough firmness to keep them from becoming an indigo mash when you bit into them, yet were supple, velvety, and delicious on the tongue. And the guacamole was creamy, chunky, and savory all at once. The fact that I got to wash this wonder down with gulps of Joni's French roast was just unfair to other food.

I got a call.

It was my manager, Eileen Stringer. A few years back, she had left the casting biz and joined a talent management agency. And she sure had kept me in mind after all.

I had to meet with her and my lawyer to sign some papers.

I finished my coffee, jumped in my car, and drove due east, toward Santa Monica, where I picked up Eileen and headed to my lawyer's office. There I signed reams of papers that guaranteed me a life well beyond the expectations of someone who had recently been living in a near-windowless basement apartment.

Eileen and I decided to celebrate.

We cruised down to Montana and Tenth, to the gastropub known as Father's Office, which I'd been wanting to check out. The chef, Sang Yoon, is sort of a culinary luminary in LA, and his restaurant has become one of the pillars of casual dining in Los Angeles largely on the backs of Yoon's famed burger and other high-quality small plates served at reasonable prices. Father's Office is usually packed solid and today was no different. Hipsters, neighborhood peeps, and foodies crowded the loud brick-and-wood room.

Beer is a crucial part of the experience at Father's Office (or FO). It goes through special surgical tubing and the variety, with 30 beers on tap, is incredible.

Now, I'd been warned ahead of time not to ask for any substitutions on the burger or to ask for any ketchup. Not a problem. I'd also been advised to grab *any* seat that became available, so we grabbed two stools at a wooden counter attached to the exposed brick wall. While we waited for our burgers, Eileen and I shared

FO's (justly) famous sweet potato fries and two glasses of the greatest IPA I've had in recent memory, Racer 5 from Bear Republic Brewing Company in Healdsburg, California. The sweet potato fries were the most flavorful I've ever encountered. Plus, the Cabrales and blue cheese roasted garlic aioli that they give you to dip them in is just perfect.

The burgers arrived at just the right time.

Dubbed the Office Burger, these babies are made from dry-aged sirloin and come topped with caramelized onion, applewood bacon compote, Gruyère, Maytag blue cheese, and arugula, all served on crusty French bread.

I took a bite of the burger that's been named the best in LA, and moaned. Not like the polite "Oh man, that's yummy" kind of moan, but a real, full-body "Ooooh baby, you're hitting my spot" kind of moan.

The crusty tear of fresh, hot French bread gave way to the rich juiciness of the beef and the nuttiness of the pungent blue cheese, and the onion compote was a jamlike sweet counterpoint to the intense, savory burger. And just when the richness of the burger was about to become overwhelming, I took a sip of the crisp, cold, not overly hoppy IPA and all was right with the world.

I kissed Eileen good-bye and headed to my car.

It was almost unnerving to be driving out here and not feeling like I was scrambling.

Like I was lost.

I headed east toward Los Feliz, where I met up with my old

friend Geoff to go look at the massive theater complex he was now overseeing. He gave me a tour of the place and walked me through the set-building process for a new production of *Tracers* he was working on. Then we hopped in the car and drove to Pink's Hot Dogs, a legendary frank purveyor on La Brea with a long, snaking waiting line reminiscent of the one outside Mr. Toad's Wild Ride at Disneyland. By the grace of all creatures great and small, we found a spot in its postage-stamp-size parking lot and took our places on the massive queue.

While we waited I gave a few high fives to fans, signed some autographs, and posed for a few cell phone pictures. Geoff laughed and busted my balls with a comment about me being on the cover of *Tiger Beat*. I punched him, he punched me back, and we made it through yet another switchback in the roped-off line. I told Geoff it was my treat.

"Damn! If I had known you were treating, I would have said we should go to the Ivy or Spago."

We entered the final phase of the line just as the sky turned a deep purplish blue, the remnant of sunlight filtering through the smog and haze. The hot dogs at Pink's come in many varieties, all garlicky, delicious, and amazing, and some are named in honor of celebrities. There's the Rosie O'Donnell, the Ozzy Osbourne, the Martha Stewart, even one named for LA Philharmonic conductor Gustavo Dudamel.

At the front of the line at last, we ordered two of Pink's famous, utterly fantastic chili-cheese dogs, an order of fries, and some drinks. I stared at the multicolored signs advertising the various celebrity hot dogs.

"Excuse me," I said to the woman behind the counter, "how do I go about getting one of those named after me?"

"You have to be famous first."

"Yeah, bitch, go get famous," Geoff told me, barely containing his laughter.

"I'll work on it, ma'am."

"That's nice. Step down, please."

I stepped down.

I paid.

Geoff couldn't stop laughing.

As we ate the juicy pink dogs with their thick duvets of bright orange cheese sauce and mortar-thick, rich, and slightly spicy chili, and I stared at the profusion of headshots lining the walls of the tiny dining room. Actors, singers, dancers, models, both famous and unknown, from every era, all of whom had darkened the doorway of this famed LA haunt. I thought about them, about the lives behind the glossy 8 × 10s and all the Hollywood dreamers out here—some fresh from auditions, some on the way to them; some who came here from their homes in Malibu or the Pacific Palisades to reminisce and feel nostalgic for their "lean" years, and some who came to be seen "among the people."

I thought about them all.

I thought about how things had changed for me since the first time I decided to hang a fang on a Pink's pup.

I thought about the old (and slightly out-of-focus) headshot that I no longer used.

I thought about the dreams that had brought me out to LA.

I thought about the dreams that had come true to bring me back out here.

And I realized that it is the universality of having dreams and loving life, of loving people and fabulous franks, that has brought us—all of us—from the Pitts to the Passed-Over, to this place. It is the universal language of the deliciousness of LA, at Pink's and elsewhere, that unites us all, whether struggling, successful, or somewhere in the middle.

Not all of us have stars on the Boulevard, five-picture deals, or a million bucks. We may not have a hot dog named after us. But we have our appetites, our yearning for delicious food, our wanderlust, and our dreams. And we have Los Angeles to satisfy them all.

Hooray for Hollywood.

Hints for Picking an Authentic Place over a Tourist Trap

- If you heard about it from your hotel's concierge, so did thousands of guests before you.

- Check out the license plates in the parking lot and look at the cars themselves. Weathered cars with local plates are a good sign.

- If there is an overemphasis on flashy signage that is incongruous with the neighborhood, it *could* be a local spot made good, or it could be trading on the neighborhood's cachet and just in it for the buck. Go for simple, humble signage—even older signs.

- Look for lines of people with *no cameras*. Locals will wait for a good bite, but to them it's not a destination, it's a habit. They don't need a pic of the place.

- Leave the areas of town that have the museums, stadiums, upscale hotels, and so on. The places around these locales generally cater to visitors, tourists, and travelling businesspeople. Go where the workers at these places go when they're off their shift. Consider safety when choosing where to go, but in my experience, taking a walk on the wild side usually produces the best finds.

- If a neighborhood has a specific ethnic concentration—Chinatown, Little Odessa, etc.—it usually has the most real-deal spots, because in first-generation immigrant communities, authenticity is the main concern for those seeking a taste of back home.

- Don't avoid community cookouts! Some of the best meals I've ever had were in church parking lots and VFW halls. Check your local listings.

- I've said it before and I'll say it again: If you are eating a certain nation's cuisine, it is always a good sign if people of that nationality choose to eat there. A Mexican restaurant with *no* people of Mexican descent eating there? *Es no bueno.*

- Trust your gut. My mom has always told me this, and she's right. If you feel that you're eating in a tourist trap, you usually are. No-frills, no-flash menus, décor, and so on are hard things to fake. Let your conscience and common sense be your guides. Bubba Gump Shrimp is about as Creole as I am.

ACKNOWLEDGMENTS

To my mom for always believing in me, inspiring me, and having the time to make dinner when she didn't have time to think.

To my dad for being my John Wayne, my sensei, and the man who showed me the power and poetry of the written word.

To my stepmom for helping me to always think outside the box and reminding me that fortune favors the bold.

To the members of my family who truly have been behind me—you know who you are.

To my true friends for always grounding me.

To my false friends for keeping me on my toes.

To the women who have loved me and those who have left me and made me harder and smarter.

To anyone who's ever found something of the religious or the sublime in a morsel of food.

To the Travel Channel for taking a chance and a leap of faith.

To Mary Harden, Nancy Curtis, Michael Kirsten, Scott Edwards, Kirsten Walther, Hayley Lozitsky, and Max Stubblefield for giving me countless opportunities to follow my dreams and for their guidance.

To Eileen Stringer for being equal parts velvet glove, mortar, caviar, bullwhip, and barbed wire.

To Pam Krauss for coming to Brooklyn on a Sunday, always speaking the brutal, beautiful truth, and scaring me straight.

To Michael Psaltis, a great man who has taken my chickenshit and brilliantly made chicken salad and never made me worry even when I needed to.

I am forever in your debt.

Adam Richman
2010

RESTAURANT LOCATIONS

CHAPTER 1
LOS ANGELES, CA

Callahan's Restaurant
1213 Wilshire Blvd
Santa Monica, CA 90403
(310) 394–6210

Zankou Chicken
1716 S. Sepulveda Blvd.
Los Angeles, 90025
(310) 444–0550
http://www.zankouchicken.com/

Tokyo Kaikan
500 E. 7th St.
Los Angeles, CA 90014
(213) 688–2564

CHAPTER 2
HONOLULU, HI

Aoki's Shave Ice
66-117 Kamehameha Hwy.
Haleiwa, HI 96712
(808) 637–7017
http://aokishaveice.com

Giovanni's Shrimp Truck
83 Kamehameha Hwy.
Kahuku, HI 96731
(808) 293–1839

Kahuku Superette
59-505 Kamehameha Hwy.
Kahuku, HI 96731
(808) 293–9878

**M. Matsumoto
Grocery Store**
66-087 Kamehameha Hwy.
Haleiwa, HI 96712
(808) 637–4827
www.matsumotoshaveice.com

CHAPTER 3
BROOKLYN, NY

Franny's
295 Flatbush Ave.
Brooklyn, NY 11217
(718) 230–0221
http://www.frannysbrooklyn.com/

L & B Spumoni Gardens
2725 86th St.
Brooklyn, NY 11223
(718) 372–8400
http://www.spumonigardens.com/
home.html

Lucali Brick Oven
575 Henry St.
Brooklyn, NY 11231
(718) 858–4086

**Pino's La Forchetta
Pizzeria**
181 7th Ave.
Brooklyn, NY 11215
(718) 965–4020

Sahadi's Specialty and Fine Foods

187 Atlantic Ave.
Brooklyn, NY 11201
(718) 624–4550
http://sahadis.com/

Totonno's Pizzeria Napolitano

1524 Neptune Ave.
Brooklyn, NY 11224
(718) 372–8606
http://www.totonnos.com

CHAPTER 4
ST. LOUIS, MO

Big Sky Café

47 S. Old Orchard Ave.
Webster Groves, MO 63119
(314) 962–5757
www.bigskycafe.net

Charlie Gitto's on the Hill

5226 Shaw Ave.
St Louis, MO 63110
(314) 772–8898
http://www.charliegittos.com/

Delmar Restaurant and Lounge

6235 Delmar Blvd
Saint Louis, MO 63130
(314) 725–6565

The Drunken Fish Sushi Restaurant & Lounge

1 Maryland Plaza
Saint Louis, MO 63108
(314) 367–4222
http://www.drunkenfish.com/

Fitz's American Grill and Bottling Works

6605 Delmar Blvd.
St Louis, MO 63130
(314) 726–9555
http://www.Fitzsrootbeer.com

Imo's Pizza

1828 Washington Ave
St. Louis, MO 63103
(314) 241–6000
http://www.imospizza.com/

Nobu's Japanese Restaurant

8643 Olive Blvd.
Saint Louis, MO 63132
(314) 997–2303
http://nobustl.com/

Oldani Brothers' Sausage Company

2201 Edwards St.
St. Louis, MO 63110
(314) 772–2125
http://www.oldanisalami.com/

Rue 13

1331 Washington Ave.
St Louis, MO 63103
(314) 588–7070
http://www.rue13stl.com

Sekisui

3024 South Grand Blvd.
St Louis, MO 63118
(314) 772–0002
http://www.sekisuiusa.com/web/

Sub Zero Vodka Bar

308 N. Euclid Ave.
St. Louis, MO 63108
314. 367. 1200
http://subzerovodkabar.com

Wasabi Sushi Bar

1228 Washington Ave
St Louis, MO 63103
(314) 421–3500
http://www.wasabistl.com

Yoshi's Sushi Bar

1637 Clarkson Rd.
Chesterfield, MO 63017
(636) 536–7778

CHAPTER 5
CLEVELAND, OH

Great Lakes Brewing Company

2516 Market Ave.
Cleveland, Ohio 44113
(216) 771–4404
http://www.greatlakesbrewing.com/

Ha Ahn Korean Restaurant

3030 Superior Ave. E
Cleveland, OH 44114
(216) 664–1152

Inn on Coventry

2785 Euclid Heights Blvd. Ste. 2
Cleveland, OH 44106
(216) 371–1811

Li Wah

2999 Payne Ave. Ste. 102
Cleveland, OH 44114
(216) 696–6556
http://liwahrestaurant.com/

Siam Café

3951 Saint Clair Ave. NE
Cleveland, OH 44114
(216) 361–2323

Superior Pho

3030 Superior Ave.
Ste E
Cleveland, OH 44114
(216) 781–7462

West Side Market

1979 W 25th St.
Cleveland, OH 44113
(216) 664–3386
http://www.westsidemarket.org/

Wonton Gourmet and BBQ

3211 Payne Ave.
Cleveland, OH 44114
(216) 875–7000

CHAPTER 6
AUSTIN, TX

Azul Tequila

4211 S Lamar Blvd., Ste. A2
Austin, TX 78704
(512) 416–9667
http://azultequila.com/

Casino el Camino

517 E 6th St.
Austin, TX 78701
512) 469–9330
http://www.casinoelcamino.net/

Mighty Cone

1600 S Congress Ave.
Austin, TX 78704
(512) 383–9609
http://www.mightycone.com/

Moonshine Patio Bar and Grill

303 Red River St.
Austin, TX 78701
(512) 236–9599
http://www.moonshinegrill.com/

Stubb's Bar-B-Q

801 Red River St.
Austin, Texas 78701
(512) 480–8341
http://www.stubbsaustin.com

CHAPTER 7
SAN FRANCISCO, CA

Acme Bread Company

1 Ferry Building, Ste 15
San Francisco, CA 94111
(415) 288–2978

The Alembic

1725 Haight St.
San Francisco, CA 94117
(415) 666–0822
http://www.alembicbar.com/

Blue Bottle Coffee

1 Ferry Building, Ste 7
San Francisco, CA 94111
(415) 983–8000
http://www.bluebottlecoffee.net/

Boccalone

1 Ferry Building, Ste 21
San Francisco, CA 94111
415) 433–6500
http://www.boccalone.com/

Cowgirl Creamery

1 Ferry Building, Ste 17
San Francisco, CA 94111
(415) 362–9354
http://www.cowgirlcreamery.com/

Nopalito

306 Broderick St
San Francisco, CA 94117
(415) 437–0303
http://www.nopalitosf.com/

CHAPTER 8
PORTLAND, ME

Becky's Diner

390 Commercial St
Portland, ME 04101
(207) 773–7070
www.beckysdiner.com/

Bob's Seafood

901 Roosevelt Trail
Windham, ME 04062
(207) 893–2882
http://www.lobsters-shipped.com/
index.html

The Fisherman's Catch Fresh Seafood Market/ The Galley Restaurant

1270 Roosevelt Trail
Raymond, ME 04071
(207) 655–4405
http://www.catchthegalley.com/

The Fishermen's Grill/The Fishermen's Net

849 Forest Ave
Portland, ME 04103
(207) 699–5657

J's Oyster

5 Portland Pier
Portland, ME 04101
(207) 772–4828
www.jsoyster.com

Lobster Shack at Two Lights

225 Two Lights Road
Cape Elizabeth, Maine 04107
(207) 799–1677
http://lobstershacktwolights.com/

Portland Lobster Company

180 Commercial St.
Portland, ME 04101
(207) 775–2112
http://portlandlobstercompany.com/

CHAPTER 9
SAVANNAH, GA

Huey's on the River

115 E River St.
Savannah, GA 31401
(912) 234–7385

Mrs. Wilkes' Dining Room

107 W Jones St.
Savannah, GA 31401
(912) 232–5997
http://www.mrswilkes.com/

Smoke Station BBQ

6724 Waters Ave.
Savannah, GA 31406
(912) 354–2524

Sweet Potatoes Kitchen

6825 Waters Ave.
Savannah, GA 31406
(912) 352–3434
http://www.toucancafe.com/sweetP.
html

Tubby's Tank House

115 E River St.
Savannah, GA 31401
(912) 233–0770

Walls' BBQ

515 E York St.
Savannah, GA 31401
(912) 232–9754

**Zunzi's Takeout
and Catering**

108 E York St.
Savannah, GA 31401
(912) 443–9555
http://www.zunzis.com/

CHAPTER 10
LOS ANGELES, CA

Father's Office

3229 Helms Ave.
Los Angeles, CA 90034
(310) 736–2224
http://www.fathersoffice.com

Joni's Coffee

552 Washington Blvd.
Marina Del Rey, CA 90292
(310) 305–7147
http://joniscoffee.com/

Katsuya

6300 Hollywood Blvd.
Los Angeles, CA 90028
(323) 871–8777

Pink's Hot Dogs

709 N La Brea Ave.
Los Angeles, CA 90038
(323) 931–4223
http://www.pinkshollywood.com

Taqueria Don Adrian

14902 Victory Blvd.
Van Nuys, CA 91411
(818) 786–0328

Versailles

10319 Venice Blvd.
Los Angeles, CA 90034
(310) 558–3168
http://versaillescuban.com

INDEX

ABOUT THE AUTHOR

Adam Richman grew up in the culinary Mecca of New York City and began a lifelong love affair with food at an early age. His enthusiasm for all things edible drew him into the culinary world after graduation, and he has held countless positions, from sandwich maker to sushi chef, at restaurants from coast to coast. After earning a master's degree in fine arts from Yale University School of Drama, Adam traveled the United States, acting in regional theaters. In 2008, he began hosting *Man v. Food* for the Travel Channel, which quickly became their highest rated show, while continuing to appear in New York theatrical productions and in television dramatic series. He currently makes his home in Brooklyn, New York.